Henry H. Hadley

Rescue Songs

the only book of songs specially adapted for rescue work - also suitable for revival services and missions

Henry H. Hadley

Rescue Songs

the only book of songs specially adapted for rescue work - also suitable for revival services and missions

ISBN/EAN: 9783337266622

Printed in Europe, USA, Canada, Australia, Japan

Cover: Foto ©Thomas Meinert / pixelio.de

More available books at **www.hansebooks.com**

JOHN R. SWENEY, WM. J. KIRKPATRICK, R. KELSO CARTER,
GEORGE C. STEBBINS, E. O. EXCELL, W. A. OGDEN, PETER
BILLHORN, E. E. NICKERSON, WILL L. THOMPSON,
D. C. WRIGHT, R. S. ROBSON, W. G. FISCHER,
D. R. MANSFIELD, D. B. TOWNER,
JAMES McGRANAHAN.

THE ONLY BOOK OF SONGS ESPECIALLY ADAPTED FOR
RESCUE WORK.

ALSO SUITABLE FOR REVIVAL SERVICES AND MISSIONS.

PREPARED BY
COL. H. H. HADLEY.

NEW YORK:
PUBLISHED FOR THE RESCUE VOLUNTEERS.
No. 158 East 42d Street.

FOR SALE BY
S. T. GORDON & SON, 13 EAST 14th STREET.

Copyright, 1890, by H. H. Hadley.

The compiler has dedicated in this book, several selections to friends who have assisted, and in memory of others.

PREFACE.

There are more songs suitable for *rescue work* in RESCUE SONGS than in any other book, including the best from almost every source.

Many publishers, writers and composers donated the pieces asked for, and others sold them at reasonable rates.

But for this and the important fact that several hundred dollars with which to buy the music and make the plates, were contributed by good friends of missions and of rescue work, this book would have to be sold at the usual price for such books, say 35 to 50 cents per copy. Thanks to these friends, the publishers are now enabled to furnish RESCUE SONGS within the means of the poorest mission, church or Sunday-school. The thanks of all rescue workers are due to those who have made it possible to give so good a book a wide circulation where so much needed. To each one who has helped or prayed for this cheery messenger of hope and peace, is tendered (In His Name) the sincere thanks of H. H. H.

Please pray that this copy may be the means of saving some soul. See MATT. 18:19 and 1 JOHN 1:7.

RESCUE SONGS.

1. The Volunteer's Song.

R. K. C. R. KELSO CARTER.

1. A cry comes up from the darkness, A wail of ag-o-ny rolls
2. Oh, who can tell this sal-va-tion? The judgment thun-der rolls;
3. Oh, who will go to the res-cue? The world mere pit-tan-ces doles;
4. From east to west we will tell it, To all men between the poles;

Thro' the night of sin, in this world of ours, 'Tis the cry of perishing souls.
Who will bear the news of redemption down To the helpless perishing souls.
'Tis the Christian saved by redeeming love Who must help the perishing souls.
We can tell it best, we who feel it most, For we were per-ishing souls.

CHORUS.

Are you saved? ful-ly saved? Has Jesus wash'd your sins away, away?
are you saved? ful-ly saved?

Then work, brother, work; the night is coming on; Oh, work, work for souls to-day.

Copyright by R. K. CARTER, 1890.

2. Come, Sinner, Come.

*"Come unto me, all ye that labor and are heavy laden."—*Matt. 11: 28.

W. E. Witter. H. R. Palmer, by per.

1. While Jesus whispers to you, Come, sinner, come! While we are praying for you, Come, sinner, come! Now is the time to own Him, Come, sinner, come! Now is the time to know Him, Come, sinner, come!
2. Are you too heavy laden? Come, sinner, come! Jesus will bear your burden, Come, sinner, come! Jesus will not deceive you, Come, sinner, come! Jesus can now redeem you, Come, sinner, come!
3. Oh, hear His tender pleading, Come, sinner, come! Come and receive the blessing, Come, sinner, come! While Jesus whispers to you, Come, sinner, come! While we are praying for you, Come, sinner, come!

Copyright, 1879, by H. R. Palmer.

3. Burst, Ye Emerald Gates.

1 Burst, ye emerald gates, and bring
  To my raptured vision
All th' ecstatic joys that spring
  Round the bright elysian.
Lo! we lift our longing eyes,
Break, ye intervening skies,
Sons of righteousness, arise,
  Ope' the gates of Paradise.

2 Hark! the thrilling symphonies,
  Seem methinks to seize us,
Join we in the holy lays,
  Jesus came to save us!
Sweetest sound in seraph's song,
Sweetest note on mortal tongue,
Sweetest carol ever sung,
  Let its echoes flow along.

5. I Believe Jesus Saves.

NEWTON. *In Memory of my Father.* J. P. WEBSTER.

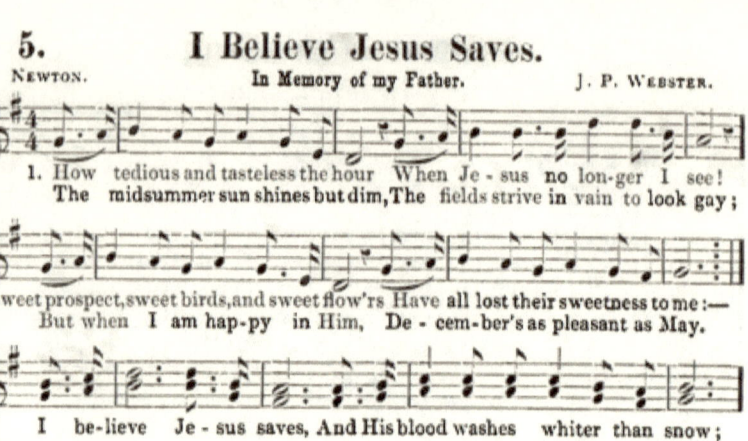

1. How tedious and tasteless the hour When Jesus no longer I see!
The midsummer sun shines but dim, The fields strive in vain to look gay;
Sweet prospect, sweet birds, and sweet flow'rs Have all lost their sweetness to me:—
But when I am happy in Him, December's as pleasant as May.

I believe Jesus saves, And His blood washes whiter than snow;
I believe Jesus saves, And His blood washes whiter than snow.

2 His name yields the richest perfume,
  And sweeter than music His voice;
His presence disperses my gloom,
  And makes all within me rejoice.
I should, were He always thus nigh,
  Have nothing to wish or to fear;
No mortal so happy as I,
  My summer would last all the year.

3 Content with beholding His face,
  My all to His pleasure resigned,
No changes of season or place
  Would make any change in my mind:

While blest with a sense of His love,
  A palace a toy would appear:
And prisons would palaces prove,
  If Jesus would dwell with me there.

4 My Lord! if indeed I am Thine,
  If Thou art my Son, and my Song,
Say,—why do I languish and pine,
  And why are my winters so long?
O! drive those dark clouds from my sky;
  Thy soul-cheering presence restore;
Or take me to Thee upon high,
  Where winter and clouds are no more.

6. My Brethren, I Have Found.

In Memory of John B. LaRue.

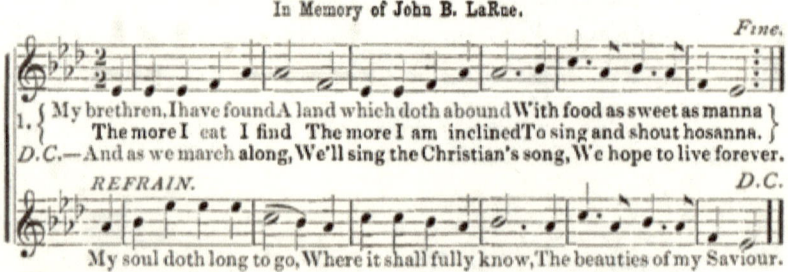

1. My brethren, I have found A land which doth abound With food as sweet as manna
   The more I eat I find The more I am inclined To sing and shout hosanna.
D.C.—And as we march along, We'll sing the Christian's song, We hope to live forever.

REFRAIN.

My soul doth long to go, Where it shall fully know, The beauties of my Saviour.

2 What must the fountain be
  From which grace flows so free,
    It yields both peace and **pleasure**;
  There's no terrestrial bliss
  Could ever equal this,
    A foretaste of my Saviour.

3 Now, brethren, can you say,
  That you are on your way—
    Are on your way to glory?
  I care not for your name;
  Religion is the same;
    Come tell the pleasing **story**.

7. Let Jesus Walk the Waves to Thee.

Rev. F. Bottome, D. D.   John Stevenson.

1. The home is sad that once was gay With laughter's mer-ry ring; And mid-night gloom o'er o - pen day Has spread her sa - ble wing. The curse has press'd her i - ron heel On in - no-cence and truth; And ev - ery hope that sense can feel Is crushed in bud - ding youth.

2. The asp has palsied manhood's strength, The senseless arm lies still; And yield - ing will is left at length With-out the power to will. The blight is on the ten-der flow'r, The worm is at the core; And bit - ter wail-ing marks the hour, While death is at the door.

3. Yet may we not in mute despair, Hang down our head and sigh; Tho' lowering clouds hang everywhere, There's brightness in the sky; There's power to break the captive's chain, There's freedom for the slave; There's life to raise the dead a - gain, For Je - sus lives to save.

4. O, man, dash down the fa - tal bowl, And look for help to heaven; There's mer - cy for the sin-sick soul, And strength to weakness giv'n :— His voice that calms the roar-ing sea, And bids the tem-pest cease; O let Him walk the waves to thee, And bid thee be at peace.

Copyright, 1890, by H. H. Hadley.

10. Redeemed, Praise the Lord!

ABBIE MILLS. WM. J. KIRKPATRICK.

By permission of JOHN J. HOOD.

1 O happy day! what a Saviour is mine!
　I am redeemed, praise the Lord!
All to His pleasure I gladly resign,
　I am redeemed, praise the Lord!

Key of C last four lines of each verse.

Jesus has taken my burden away;
　Jesus has turned all my night into day,
Jesus has come to my heart—come to stay,
　I am redeemed, praise the Lord!—CHO.

Use first four lines as Chorus.

2 Thanks be to God for the great vict'ry given,
　I am redeemed, praise the Lord!
Now I am free; every chain has been riven,—
　I am redeemed, praise the Lord!
Out of the pit and the mire and the clay,
　Jesus has borne me in triumph away;
Safe on the rock I am standing to-day—
　I am redeemed, praise the Lord!—CHO.

3 O, clap your hands, all ye people of God,
　I am redeemed, praise the Lord!
Let ev'ry tongue speak His mercy abroad,
　I am redeemed, praise the Lord!
His loving kindness is better than gold;
　He doth bestow more than my cup can hold;
Wondrous salvation, that ne'er can be told,
　I am redeemed, praise the Lord!—CHO.

4 Glory to God, I would shout evermore,
　I am redeemed, praise the Lord!
O for a voice that could reach every shore,
　I am redeemed, praise the Lord!
Help me, ye ransomed, awake every string,
　Let earth rejoice and the whole heavens ring,
While we the chorus unitedly sing,
　I am redeemed, praise the Lord!—CHO.

Words and Music in "Precious Hymns." JOHN. J. HOOD, Pub., Phil.

12. Weep For The Fallen.

"Every eight minutes a drunkard dies in America."

1. Weep for the fall-en! hang your heads in sor-row, And mourn-ful-ly sing the requiem sad and slow. Thousands have perished by the fell de-stroy-er; Oh weep for youth and beau-ty, Oh weep for youth and beau-ty, Oh weep for youth and beau-ty in the grave laid low!

2. Voic-es of wail-ing tell of hope-less anguish, While sor-row-ing mothers bid us on-ward go. Hark! to their ac-cents, theirs the brok-en-heart-ed, Who weep for youth and beau-ty, Who weep for youth and beau-ty, Who weep for youth and beau-ty in the grave laid low!

3 Hear how they bid us sound the timely warning,
   While yet there is hope to shun the cup of woe;
For is it nothing, ye who see no danger,
   To weep for youth and beauty in the grave laid low?

4 Weep for the fallen; but amid your sorrow,
   Still point to the cross that freedom can bestow;
Rescue, dear Saviour, from the fell destroyer,
   For why should youth and beauty in the grave lie low?

13. Royal Way of the Cross.

By per. of PHILIP PHILLIPS.
Rev. L. HARTSOUGH.

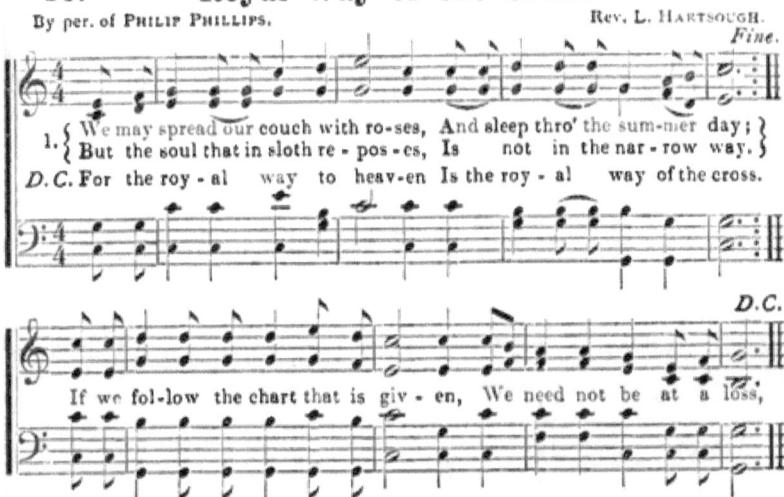

1. We may spread our couch with ro-ses, And sleep thro' the sum-mer day;
But the soul that in sloth re-pos-es, Is not in the nar-row way.
D.C. For the roy-al way to heav-en Is the roy-al way of the cross.

If we fol-low the chart that is giv-en, We need not be at a loss,

2 To one who is rear'd in splendor,
    The cross is a heavy load,
   And the feet that are soft and tender,
    Will shrink from the thorny road:
   But the chains of the soul must be riven,
    And wealth must be as dross;
   For the royal way to heaven
    Is the royal way of the cross.

3 We say we will walk to-morrow
    The path we refuse to-day,
   And still with our lukewarm sorrow
    We shrink from the narrow way.
   What heeded the chosen eleven,
    How the fortunes of life might toss,
   As they followed their Master to heaven
    By the royal way of the cross?

14. The Gracious Call.

TUNE,—HORTON.
WARTENSEE.

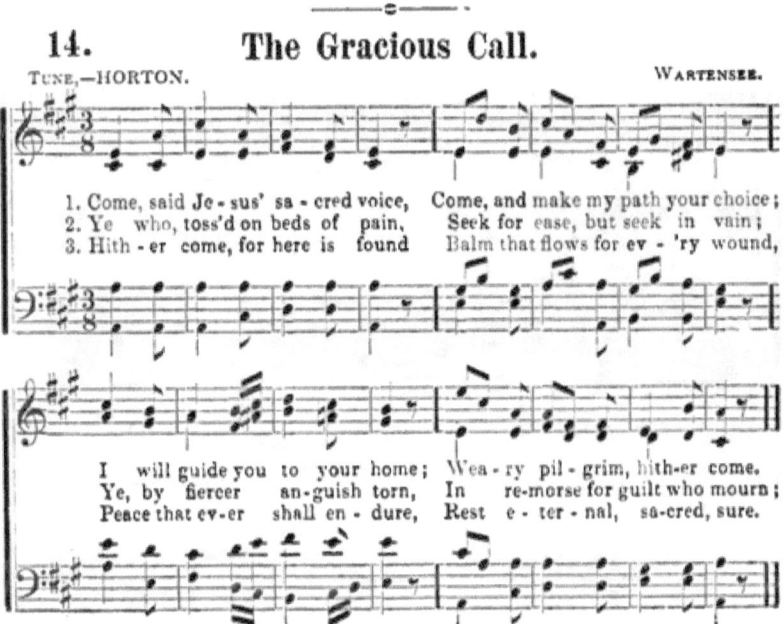

1. Come, said Je-sus' sa-cred voice, Come, and make my path your choice;
2. Ye who, toss'd on beds of pain, Seek for ease, but seek in vain;
3. Hith-er come, for here is found Balm that flows for ev-'ry wound,

I will guide you to your home; Wea-ry pil-grim, hith-er come.
Ye, by fiercer an-guish torn, In re-morse for guilt who mourn;
Peace that ev-er shall en-dure, Rest e-ter-nal, sa-cred, sure.

Redemption. Concluded.

is thy sting, Oh! death? And where is now thy vict'ry boasting grave?

5 He comes in lovely dress
   Of perfect righteousness,
To clothe me in the garments of the King;
   That, free from sin and death,
   I may, with ransomed breath,
Hosannah in the highest, shout and sing.

6 Then, though the day be long,
   I'll sing the battle-song,
That Jesus is a Victor in the fight.

In Him, I love to tell,
I conquer death and hell;
I live by faith, and walk no more by sight.

7 Oh! let the heavens ring,
   And every creature sing.
Salvation now, and Righteousness is He;
   On earth and heaven's shore
   I'll praise Him evermore;
He's Wisdom and Redemption now to me.

16. Whosoever Will May Come.

R. K. C.   R. Kelso Carter.

1. Come to Jesus now, the invitation hear, For he came to call the wand'rers home;
2. Do not heed the world's alluring siren song, Sin will ever grow more burdensome;
3. See the cloud of witnesses beyond the strife, Who for Christ have suffered martyr-[dom;

Turn a-side from sin, and cast away all fear, The spirit and the Bride say, Come!
Set your face to heaven with a purpose strong, Let him that heareth, now say, Come!
See the flowing fountain of e-ter-nal life, Let him that is athirst now come.

Cho.—Free to all the gracious in-vi-ta-tion stand's For whosoever will may come.

CHORUS.   D.S.

Jesus saves! Jesus saves! Praise the Lord! for all He saves us from.
Jesus saves! Jesus saves! Praise the Lord!

Copyright by R. K. CARTER. 1890.

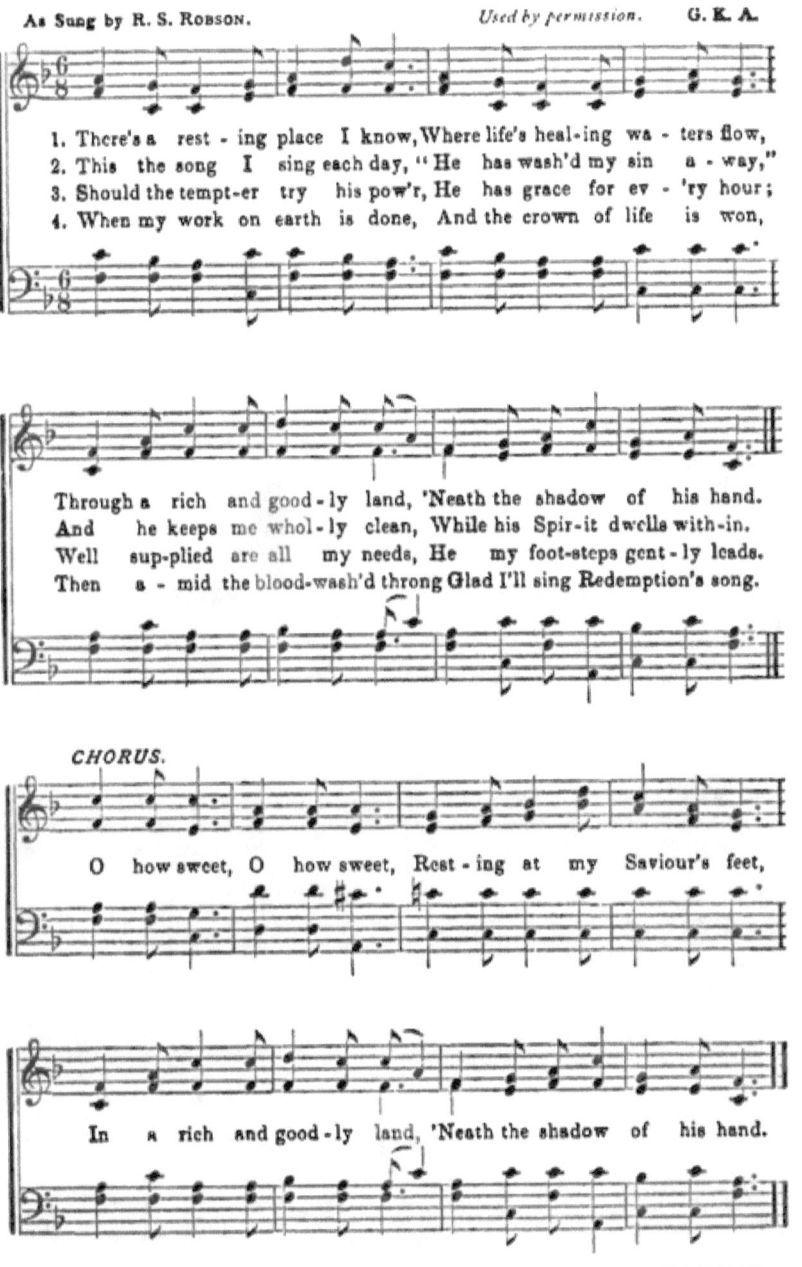

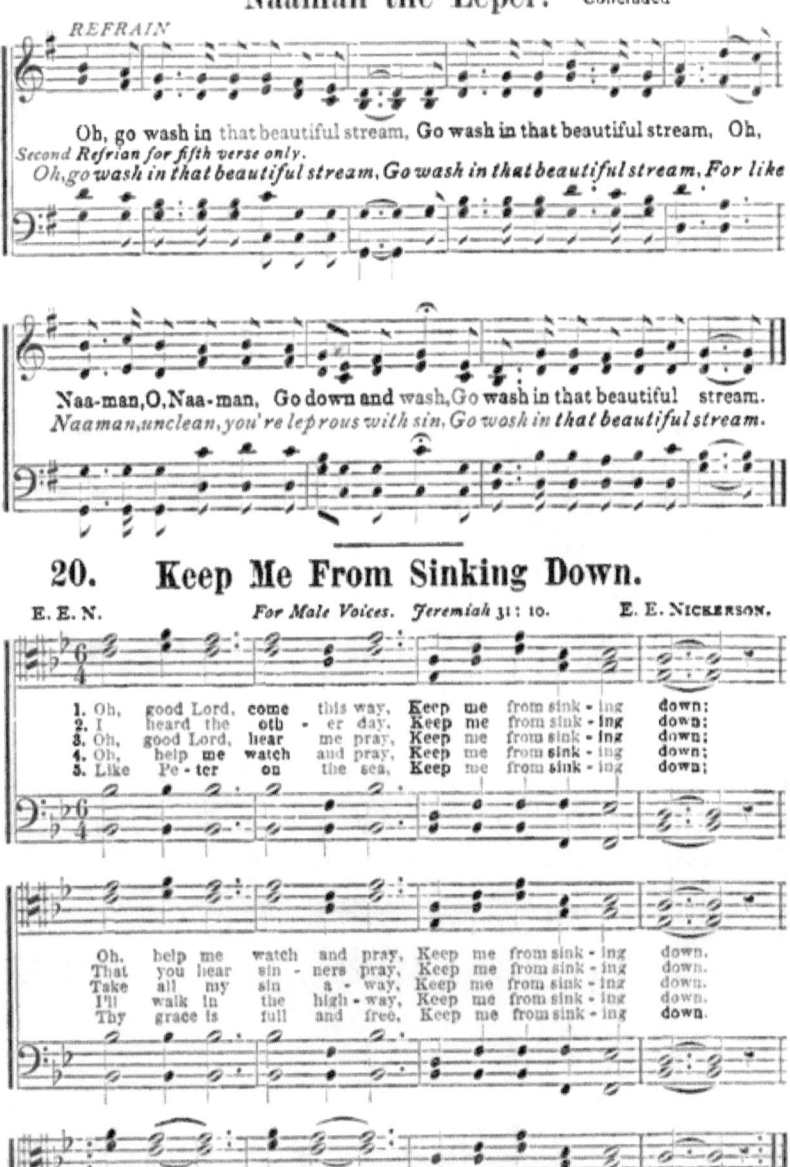

21. We Walk by Faith.

Words by FANNY J. CROSBY.   Used by permission.   Music by WM. J. KIRKPATRICK.

We walk by faith, etc.

1. We walk by faith.......... and O how sweet........ The flow'rs that
2. We walk by faith.......... He wills it so,.......... And marks the
3. We walk by faith.......... di-vine-ly blest,.......... On Him we
4. And thus by faith.......... till life shall end..........We'll walk with

grow........ beneath our feet......And fragrance breathe........ a-long the
path........ that we should go;......And when, at times........ our sky is
lean,........ in Him we rest;......The more we trust........ our Shepherd's
Him,........ our dearest Friend,... Till safe we tread...... the fields of

way........ That leads the soul.......... to end-less day........
dim,........ He gent-ly draws.......... us close to Him........
care,........ The more His love.......... 'tis ours to share........
light,........ Where faith is lost.......... in per-fect sight........

CHORUS.

We walk by faith, but not a-lone, Our Shepherd's ten-der voice we hear,

Copyright, 1885, by W. J. Kirkpatrick.

We Walk by Faith. Concluded.

And feel His hand within our own, And know that He is al-ways near.

22. O Happy Day.

July 28th, 1886, 9.40 p. m. At the old Jerry McAuley Mission, 316 Water St., N. Y.
PHILIP DODDRIDGE.

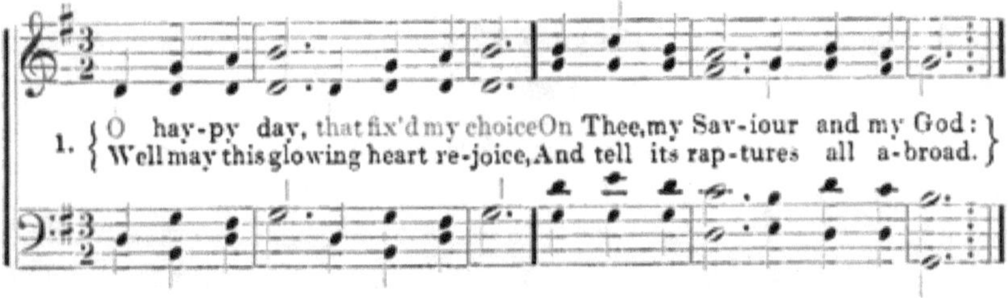

1. O hap-py day, that fix'd my choice On Thee, my Sav-iour and my God:
   Well may this glowing heart re-joice, And tell its rap-tures all a-broad.

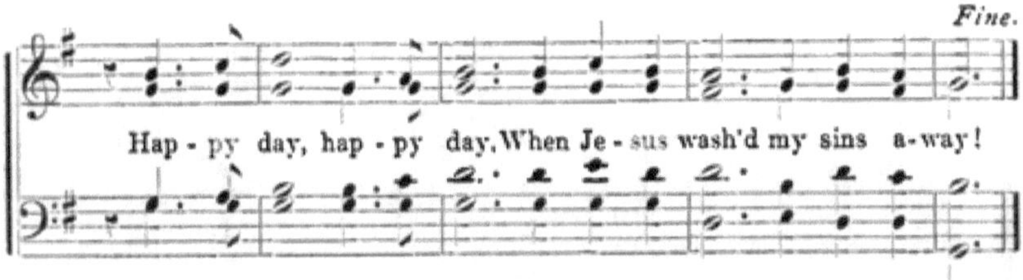

Fine.
Hap-py day, hap-py day, When Je-sus wash'd my sins a-way!

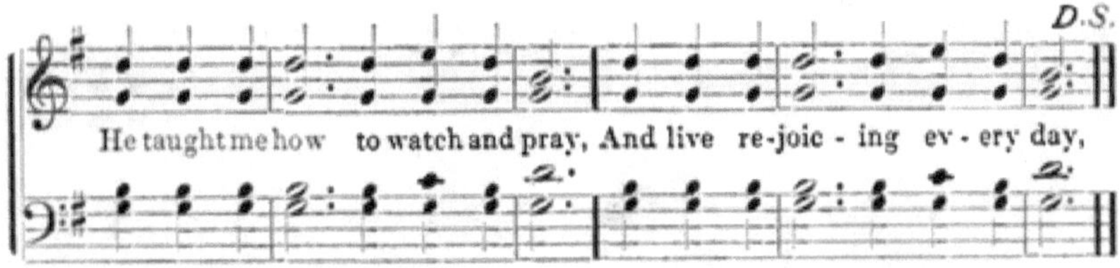

D.S.
He taught me how to watch and pray, And live re-joic-ing ev-ery day,

2 O happy bond, that seals my vows
   To Him who merits all my love!
Let cheerful anthems fill His house,
   While to that sacred shrine I move.

3 'Tis done! the great transaction's done!
   I am my Lord's, and He is mine:
He drew me, and I follow'd on,
   Charmed to confess the voice divine.

4 Now rest, my long-divided heart;
   Fix'd on this blissful centre, rest;
Nor ever from thy Lord depart;
   With Him, of every good possessed.

5 High Heaven that heard the solemn vow,
   That vow renew'd shall daily hear,
Till in life's latest hour I bow,
   And bless in death a bond so dear.

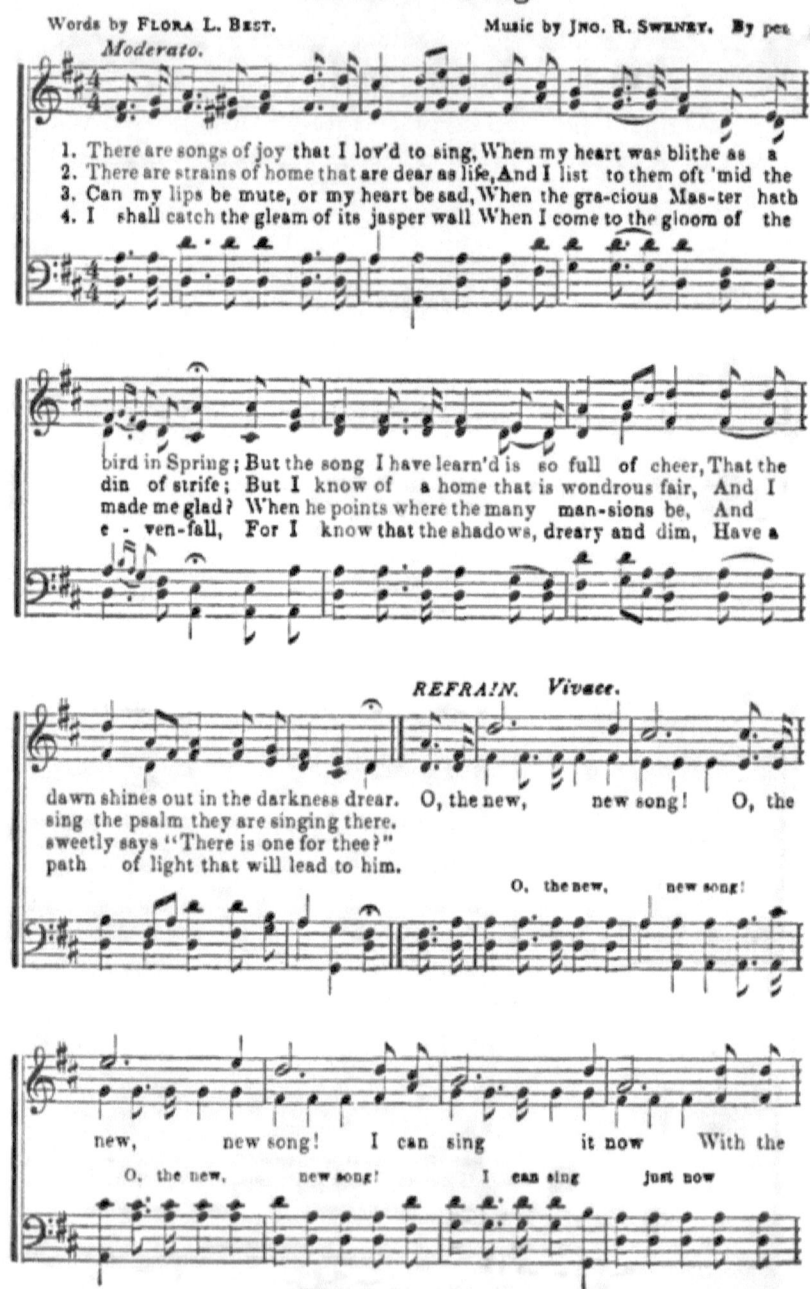

The New Song. Concluded.

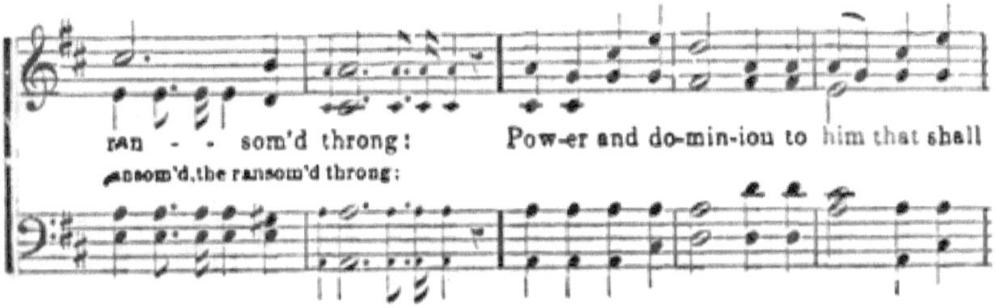

ran - - som'd throng: Pow-er and do-min-ion to him that shall
ransom'd, the ransom'd throng;

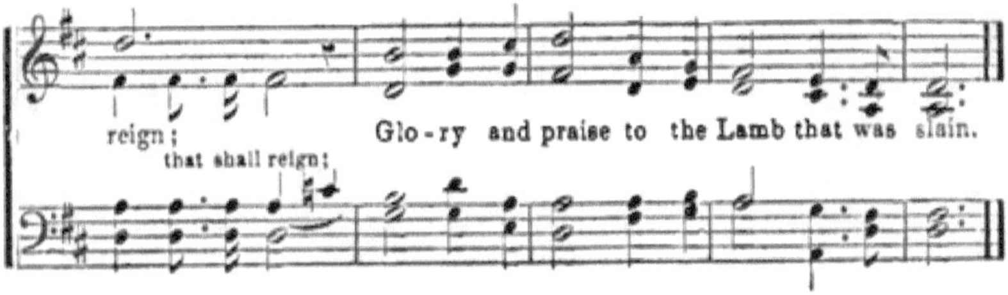

reign; Glo-ry and praise to the Lamb that was slain.
that shall reign;

---

24 Consolation.

MARY SMALL.   GEO. E. LEE.

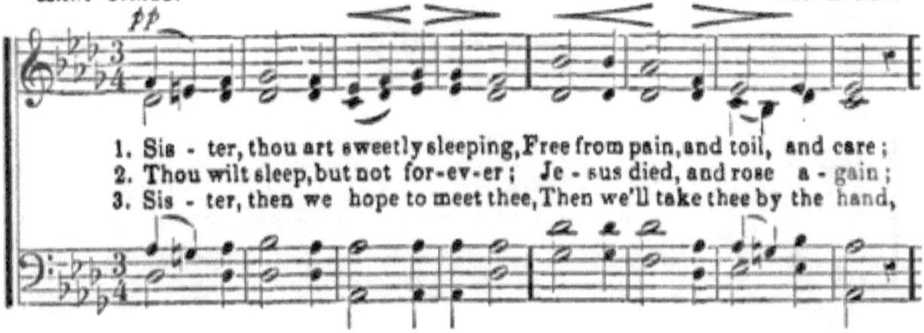

1. Sis - ter, thou art sweetly sleeping, Free from pain, and toil, and care;
2. Thou wilt sleep, but not for-ev-er; Je - sus died, and rose a - gain;
3. Sis - ter, then we hope to meet thee, Then we'll take thee by the hand,

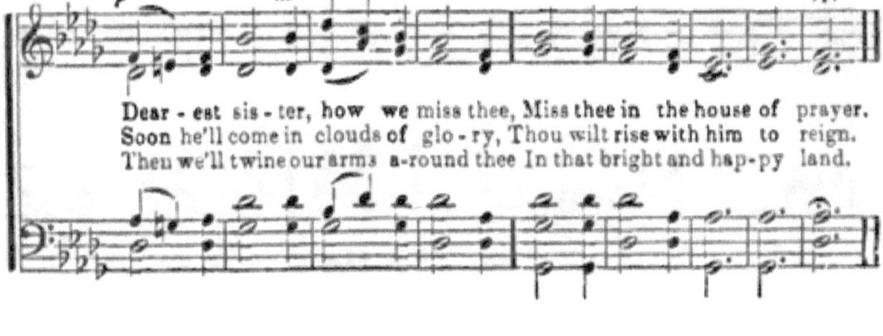

Dear - est sis - ter, how we miss thee, Miss thee in the house of prayer.
Soon he'll come in clouds of glo - ry, Thou wilt rise with him to reign.
Then we'll twine our arms a-round thee In that bright and hap-py land.

25. Welcome for Me.

Fanny J. Crosby.   W. J. Kirkpatrick.

1. Like a bird on the deep, far away from its nest, I had wander'd, my Saviour from Thee; But Thy dear loving voice call'd me home to Thy breast, And I knew there was welcome for me.
2. I am safe in the ark; I have folded my wings On the bosom of mercy divine; I am filled with the light of Thy presence so bright, And the joy that will ever be mine.

CHORUS.
Welcome for me, Saviour from Thee; A smile and a welcome for me; Now, like a dove, I rest in Thy love, And find a sweet refuge in Thee, in Thee.

3 I am safe in the ark, and I dread not the storm,
   Though around me the surges may roll;
   I will look to the skies, where the day never dies,
   I will sing of the joy in my soul.

Copyright, 1885, by W. J. Kirkpatrick. Used by purchase of right.

26. Away Over Jordan.

As Sung by Alice Terrell.   E. E. Nickerson.

1. Oh, we are going to wear a crown, To wear a starry crown.
2. You must repent, to wear a crown, To wear a starry crown.

Oh, we are going to wear a crown, To wear a starry crown.
You must repent, to wear a crown, To wear a starry crown.

CHORUS.
Away over Jordan, With my blessed Jesus,
Away over Jordan, To wear a starry crown.

27. WHEN PEACE LIKE A RIVER.

1 When peace, like a river, attendeth my way,
   When sorrows, like sea billows roll,
  Whatever my lot, thou hast taught me to say—
   It is well, it is well with my soul.
  Chorus.—It is well with my soul,
    It is well, it is well with my soul.
2 Though Satan should buffet, though trials should come,
   Let this blest assurance control,
  That Christ hath regarded my helpless estate,
   And hath shed his own blood for my soul.
3 My sin—oh the bliss of this glorious thought—
   My sin—not in part, but the whole,
  Is nailed to his cross, and I bear it no more,
   Praise the Lord, praise the Lord, oh my soul!
4 And Lord, haste the day when the faith shall be sight,
   The clouds be rolled back as a scroll;
  The trump shall resound, and the Lord shall descend,
   "Even so,"—it is well with my soul.

29. Shall I be Saved To-night.

FANNY J. CROSBY.   MRS. M. BLISS WILSON. By per.

1. Je-sus is pleading with my poor soul, Shall I be saved to-night?
2. Je-sus was nailed to the cross for me, Shall I be saved to-night?
3. Je-sus is knock-ing at my poor heart, Shall I be saved to-night?
4. What if that voice I should hear no more, Shall I be saved to-night?

If I be-lieve, He will make me whole, Shall I be saved to-night?
How can my heart so un-grate-ful be? Shall I be saved to-night?
What if His Spir-it should now de-part? Shall I be saved to-night?
Quickly I'll o-pen this bolt-ed door, Save me, O Lord, to-night.

Ten-der-ly, sad-ly I hear Him say, How can you grieve me from day to day?
Now He will save me by grace divine, Now, if I will, I may call Him mine;
O-ver and o-ver His voice I hear, Sweet-ly it falls on my list'ning ear;
Bless-ed Re-deem-er, come in, come in, Pi-ty my sorrow, forgive my sin?

Shall I go on in the old, old way, Or shall I be saved to-night?
Can I the pleasures of earth re-sign? Oh, shall I be saved to-night?
Shall I re-ject Him—a friend so dear? Oh, shall I be saved to-night?
Now let Thy work in my soul be-gin, For I will be saved to-night.

30. Sinner, See Yon Light.

J. C. BATEMAN.

1. Sinner, see yon light Shining clear and bright From the Cross on Cal-va-ry, Where the Saviour died, And from His side Came the Blood that sets us free.
2. In the gloomy shade When He knelt and pray'd, Oh, what painful ag-o-ny! When His brow was wet With the bloody sweat In the gar-den of Geth-sem-a-ne.
3. See, the Saviour stands With His wounded hands, And He calls aloud to thee, Come a-way to Him And confess your sin, Come to Him who died for thee.

CHORUS.
Come a-way, come a-way, Come a-way, come a-way, To the Cross for ref-uge flee; See the Saviour stands With His bleeding hands, Thy ransom He paid on the tree.

From the "Musical Salvationist." By per.

31. Step Out on the Promise.

To John H. Murray.

Arr. by E. F. M. E. F. Miller.

1. O mourner in Zion, how blessed art thou,
2. O ye that are hungry and thirsty, rejoice!
3. Who sighs for a heart from iniquity free?
4. Step out on this promise, and Christ thou shalt win,

For Jesus, is waiting to comfort thee now,
For ye shall be filled; do you hear that sweet voice
O poor troubled soul! there's a promise for thee,
"The blood of His Son cleanseth us from all sin,"

Fear not to rely on the word of thy God;
Inviting you now to the banquet of God;
There's rest, weary one, in the bosom of God;
It cleanseth me now, hallelujah to God;

Step out on the promise,— get under the blood.
Step out on the promise,— get under the blood.
Step out on the promise,— get under the blood.
I rest on His promise,—I'm under the blood.

Copyright, 1884, by E. F. Miller. From "The Shout of Victory," by per.

He Rose. Concluded.

And the Lord shall bear my spir-it home, And the Lord shall bear my spirit home.

3 ‖: The cold grave could not hold him, nor death's cold iron bands. :‖
4 ‖: An angel came from heaven, and rolled the stone away. :‖
5 ‖: Sister Mary she came running; her Saviour for to see. :‖
6 ‖: The angel said, "He is not here, He's gone to Galilee." :‖

---

33 I Yield to Thee.

REV. FRANK POLLOCK.   CHAS. E. POLLOCK.

With expression.

1. I yield to Thee, my Father: O take this heart of stone, And give me one so
2. I yield to Thee, dear Jesus, Thy blood can peace impart; And write Thy name most
3. I yield to Thee, blest Spirit, To take the full control; Oh, sanc-ti-fy the

REFRAIN.

ten-der That it shall be Thy throne. I yield,... I yield,... I
precious Up-on my yielding heart.
pow-ers Of my poor yearning soul.   I yield,   I yield,

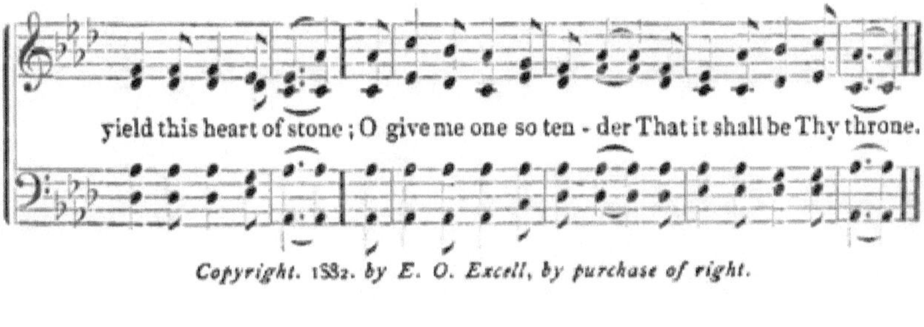

yield this heart of stone; O give me one so ten-der That it shall be Thy throne.

Copyright, 1882, by E. O. Excell, by purchase of right.

Lead me gently Home, Father. Concluded.

Lest I fall up-on the way-side, Lead me gent-ly home.
gent-ly home.

---

35. Jesus bids you Come.

W. T. L.   (*May be sung as a Solo.*)   WILL L. THOMPSON.

1. Je-sus bids you come, Je-sus bids you come:
2. Je-sus bids you come, Je-sus bids you come:
3. Je-sus bids you come, Je-sus bids you come:
4. Je-sus bids you come, Je-sus bids you come:

Earn-est-ly for you he's call-ing, Gent-ly at thy
Wea-ry trav-'ler, do not tar-ry, Je-sus will thy
Voic-es may not al-ways call you, "Late, too late," may
Where 'tis love and joy for-ev-er, Where we'll meet to

heart he's pleading, "Come un-to me, Come un-to me."
bur-dens car-ry, Oh, will you come? Oh, will you come?
yet be-fall you, "Why will ye die?" "Why will ye die?"
part, no, nev-er, Sin-ner, come home, Oh, come, come home.

By permission of W. L. THOMPSON, East Liverpool, O.

36. Bear The Cross For Jesus.

As sung by Mr. and Mrs. Wm. V. Baker, the blind Evangelists.

Arranged for "Rescue Songs."   Arr. by Mrs. K. BAKER.

1. Bear the cross for Je - sus, Bear it ev - ery day, Though the path be rug-ged, Bear it all the way; Bear the cross for Je - sus, What-so - e'er it be, Bear it and re - mem - ber, All is love for thee.
2. Bear the cross for Je - sus, Bear it thro' the strife, Or in pain and si-lence, What - so - e'er thy life. Bear the cross with patience, Though you sigh for rest, Just the one He gives you, Is for you the best.
3. Bear the cross for Je - sus, Would you know the pow'r Of His grace to save you, Save you hour by hour? Bear the cross for Je - sus, Nev - er mind its weight, We shall leave our bur - dens At the Gol - den Gate.

CHORUS.

Bear the cross, Bear the cross, Bear it ev - ery day, Bear the cross for Je - sus, Bear it all the way.

Copyright, 1890, by H. H. HADLEY.

37. Oh! 'tis Glory in My Soul.

Words by FLORA L. BEST. Music by JNO. R. SWENEY.

1. To thy cross, dear Christ, I'm clinging, All my re-fuge and my plea;
2. Long my heart hath heard thee call-ing, But I thrust a-side thy grace;
3. Love e-ter-nal, light e-ter-nal, Close me safe-ly, sweet-ly in;

Matchless is thy lov-ing kindness, Else it had not stoop'd to me.
Yet, O boundless con-de-scen-sion, Love is shin-ing from thy face.
Sav-iour, let thy balm of heal-ing Ev-er keep me free from sin.

CHORUS.

Oh, 'tis glo-ry! oh, 'tis glo-ry! Oh, 'tis glo-ry in my soul,

For I've touch'd the hem of his garment, And his pow'r doth make me whole.

37½.   OH, FOR A HEART TO PRAISE MY GOD.

1 Oh, for a heart to praise my God,
  A heart from sin set free;
  A heart that always feels the blood
  So freely spilt for me.

2 A heart resign'd, submissive, meek,
  My great Redeemer's throne:
  Where only Christ is heard to speak,
  Where Jesus reigns alone:

3 An humble, lowly, contrite heart,
  Believing, true and clean;

Which neither life nor death can part
From him that dwells within:

4 A heart in every thought renew'd,
  And full of love divine;
  Perfect and right, and pure and good,
  A copy, Lord, of thine.

5 Thy nature, gracious Lord, impart;
  Come quickly from above;
  Write thy new name upon my heart,
  Thy new best name of Love.

38. The Cross.

REV. J. H. STOCKTON. PETER R. BERGEN.

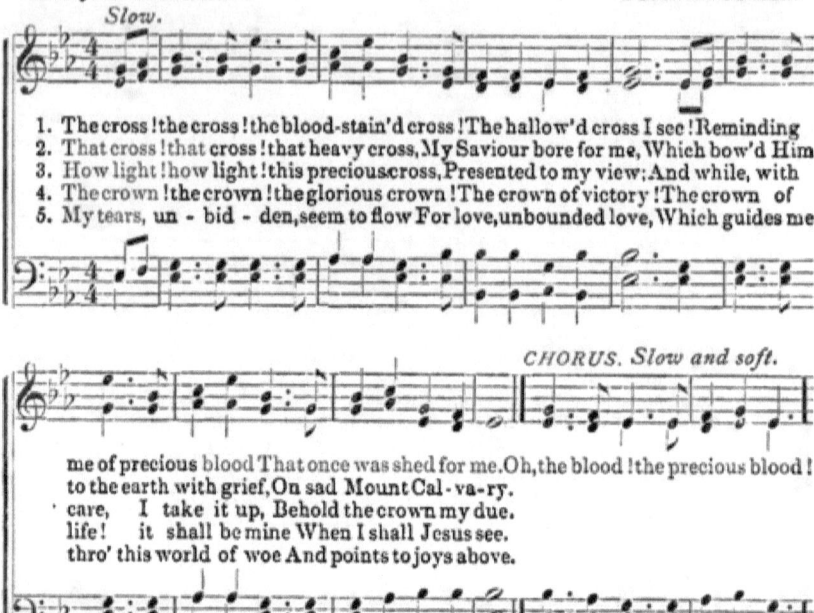

1. The cross! the cross! the blood-stain'd cross! The hallow'd cross I see! Reminding me of precious blood That once was shed for me. Oh, the blood! the precious blood! That Jesus shed for me Upon the cross, in crimson flood, Just *now* by faith I see.
2. That cross! that cross! that heavy cross, My Saviour bore for me, Which bow'd Him to the earth with grief, On sad Mount Cal-va-ry.
3. How light! how light! this precious cross, Presented to my view; And while, with care, I take it up, Behold the crown my due.
4. The crown! the crown! the glorious crown! The crown of victory! The crown of life! it shall be mine When I shall Jesus see.
5. My tears, un-bid-den, seem to flow For love, unbounded love, Which guides me thro' this world of woe And points to joys above.

39. The Lord will Provide.

PROF. S. C. HARRINGTON.

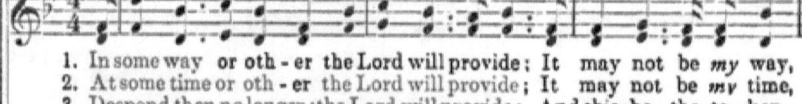

1. In some way or oth-er the Lord will provide; It may not be *my* way,
2. At some time or oth-er the Lord will provide; It may not be *my* time,
3. Despond then no longer; the Lord will provide; And this be the to-ken—
4. March on, then, right boldly; the sea shall divide; The pathway made glorious,

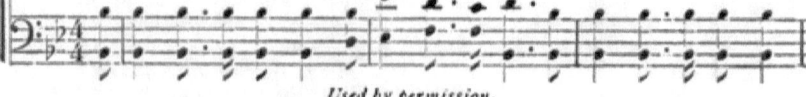

Used by permission.

The Lord will Provide. Concluded.

It may not be *thy* way, And yet, in His *own* way, "The Lord will provide."
It may not be *thy* time, And yet, in His *own* time, "The Lord will provide."
No word He hath spoken Was ev-er yet broken—"The Lord will provide."
With shoutings victorious, We'll join in the cho-rus, "The Lord will provide."

40. O, Sing of His Mighty Love.

Rev. F. Bottome.

1. { O, bliss of the pu-ri-fied! bliss of the free! I plunge in the
   O'er sin and un-clean-ness ex-ult-ing I stand, And point to the
   crim-son tide o-pened for me!
   print of the nails in His hand. }

QUARTETTE Light.

O, sing of His might-y love, Sing of His might-y love, Sing of His might-y love—mighty to save.

2 O, bliss of the purified! Jesus is mine,
No longer in dread condemnation I pine;
In conscious salvation I sing of His grace
Who lifteth upon me the smiles of His face!—*Cho.*

3 O, bliss of the purified! bliss of the pure!
No wound hath the soul that His blood cannot cure;
No sorrow-bowed head but may sweetly find rest,
No tears—but may dry them on Jesus' breast.—*Cho.*

4 O, Jesus the crucified! Thee will I sing!
My blessed Redeemer! my God, and my King!
My soul filled with rapture shall shout o'er the grave,
And triumph in death in the MIGHTY TO SAVE!

Used by permission.

I Will Shout His Praise. Concluded.

glo-ry,....... And we'll all sing hal-le-lu-jah in heaven by and by
So will I, so will I,

42. Thou Art a Mighty Saviour.

Words and Music by G. S. Smith.

p Allegro.

1. Bless-ed Lamb of Cal-va-ry, Thou hast done great things for me;
2. 'Twas for me Thy Blood was spilt, That I might be cleans'd from guilt;
3. Draw me clo-ser, Lord, to Thee, May my life a bless-ing be;

Thou didst leave Thy home a-bove, Thou didst suf-fer out of love.
In Thy mer-cy, rich and free, Thou hast pardoned ev-en me.
Now, Lord, let my light so shine That the world may know I'm Thine.

f CHORUS.

Thou art a might-y Sav-iour, Thy love doth nev-er wa-ver;
Thou shalt be mine for ev-er, And Thine a-lone I'll be.

From the "Musical Salvationist." By per.

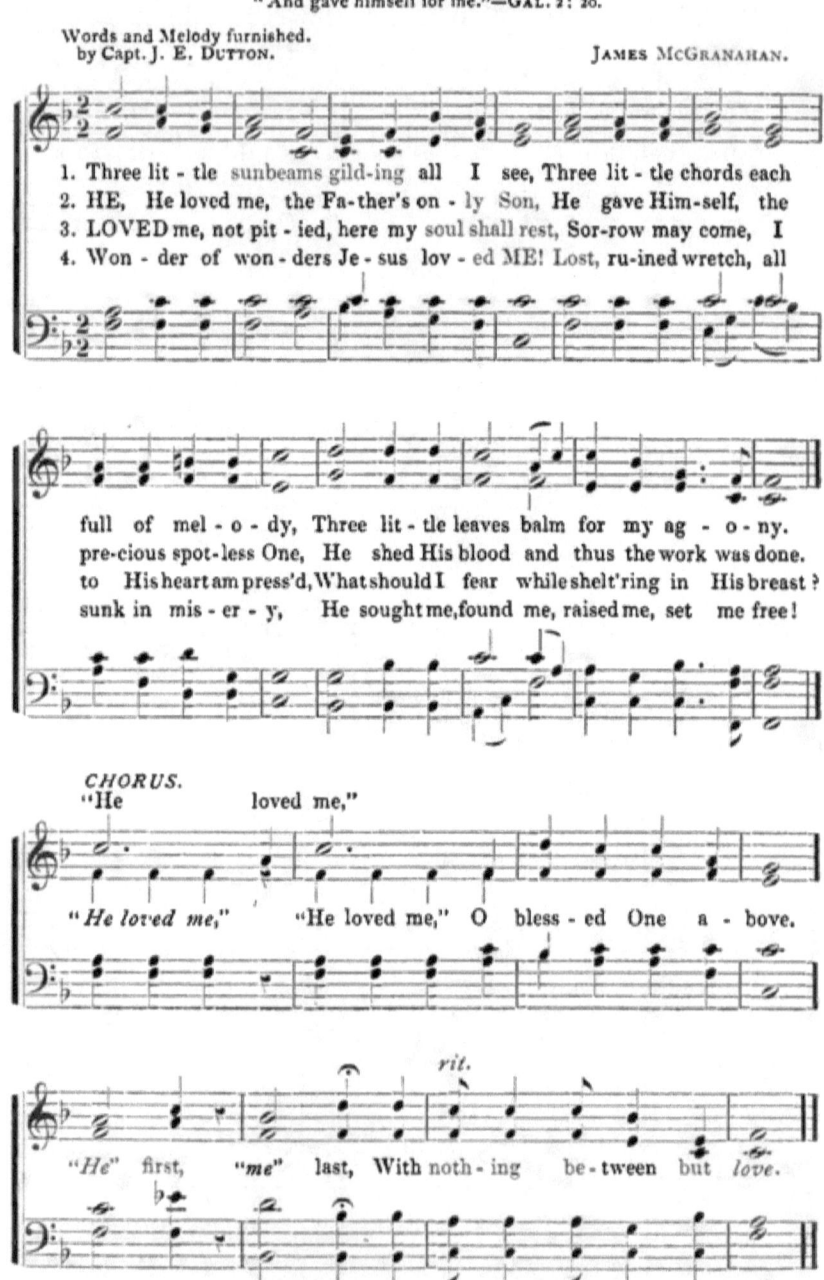

46. Wait a Little while.

H. POLLARD, 1881.
Southern Melody.
As Sung by Eld. D. R. MANSFIELD.
(Arr. by F. A. BLACKMER.)

4 When sorrow, pain and death are o'er,
  Then we'll sing the New Song,
And sighs and tears shall be no more,
  Then we'll sing the New Song.

5 When to the pearly gates we come,
  Then we'll sing the New Song;
When we have reach'd our blissful home,
  Then we'll sing the New Song.

6 When we shall tread life's river brink,
  Then we'll sing the New Song,
And of those crystal waters drink,
  Then we'll sing the New Song.

7 Where all will be immortal, fair,
  There we'll sing the New Song, [wear,
When blood-wash'd robes are ours to
  Then we'll sing the New Song.

By permission.   Copyright, 1881, by D. R. Mansfield.

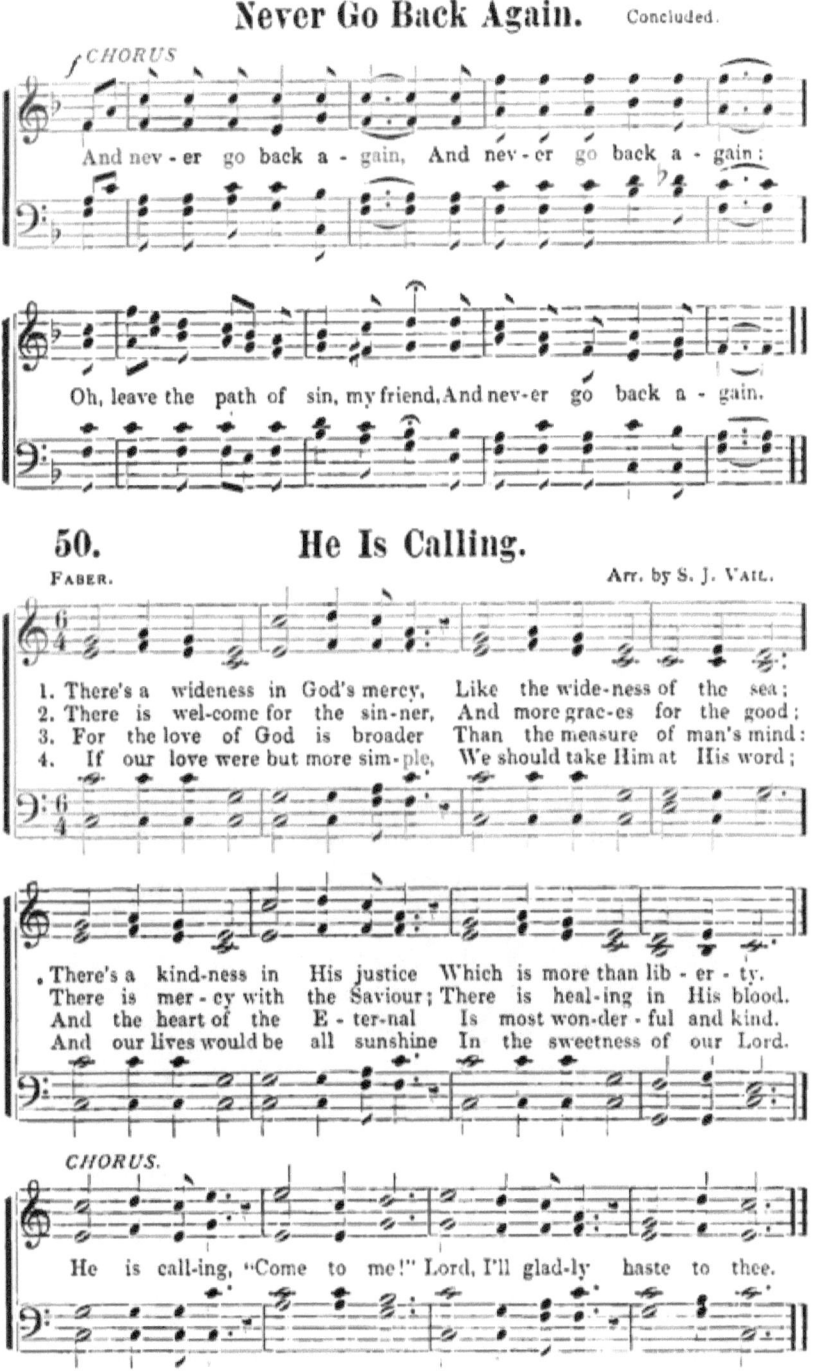

51. Hours That Are Fleeting Away.

H. H. BOOTH, by per.
S. C. SLATER.

mp Andante con moto.

1. Hours that are fleet-ing a - way, Short'ning thy time here to stay, Are bringing thee near, Thy sentence to hear, For what thou art do-ing to - day! Oh, sin-ner, make haste, There's no time to waste! Oh, sin-ner, make haste, There's no time to waste!
2. Death that is draw-ing so nigh, Asks, "Art thou read-y to die?" 'Tis eas-y to sneer When there's naught to fear, But dy-ing canst thou Him de - ny? Oh, *Death* will de-clare Thy aw-ful de-spair! Oh, *Death* will de-clare Thy aw-ful de-spair!
3. Wounded for *thee* was thy King, Smit-ten *thy* par-don to bring! En - dur-ing the scorn, The cross and the thorn, Thy poor heart of sor-row to win. From heav-en He came Thy soul to re-claim. From heaven He came Thy soul to re-claim.

mp CHORUS.

Swift - ly time rush - es by, Sin - ner, soon thou must die,

Swiftly, swiftly, Sin-ner, sinner,

Hours That Are Fleeting Away. Concluded.

Come, for soon for-ev-er, Mer-cy's gate will close.

4 Longing thy Saviour to be,
  Peace now He offers to thee;
  And pleasures untold
  He wants to unfold
  If only to Him thou wilt flee.
  ‖: Oh, joy to thy heart
  He waits to impart :‖

5 Mercy so wondrous as this,
  Sinner, be wise not to miss,
  Lest, finding, *too late*,
  Thou'rt *outside the gate*
  Of mercy, of pardon, and bliss.
  ‖: *To reach thus the tomb,*
  How awful thy doom! :‖

52. The Bleeding Lamb.

To Dr. Henry Wilson.   Arranged, W. J. K.

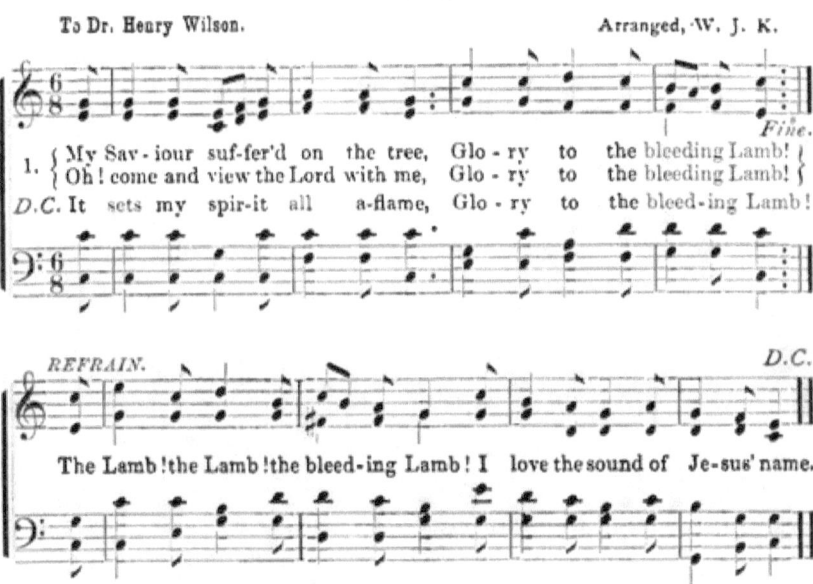

1. My Sav-iour suf-fer'd on the tree, Glo-ry to the bleeding Lamb!
   Oh! come and view the Lord with me, Glo-ry to the bleeding Lamb!
   D.C. It sets my spir-it all a-flame, Glo-ry to the bleed-ing Lamb!

REFRAIN.
The Lamb! the Lamb! the bleed-ing Lamb! I love the sound of Je-sus' name.

2 He bore my sins, and curse, and shame,
  Glory to the bleeding Lamb;
  And I am sav'd through Jesus' name,
  Glory to the bleeding Lamb.

3 I know my sins are all forgiv'n,
  Glory to the bleeding Lamb;
  And I am on my way to heav'n,
  Glory to the bleeding Lamb.

4 And when the storms of life are o'er,
  Glory to the bleeding Lamb;
  I'll sing upon a happier shore,
  Glory to the bleeding Lamb.

5 And this my ceaseless song shall be,—
  Glory to the bleeding Lamb;—
  That Jesus tasted death for me,
  Glory to the bleeding Lamb.

54. Sowing the Tares.

Dedicated to "Brother Will," M. Cell 1069.

Words by a Convict.
M. A. Lee.

Slow. To be sung as a Solo.

1. Sow-ing the tares, when it might have been wheat, Sowing of mal-ice, spite, and de-ceit, We might have sown ro-ses a-mid life's sad cares, While we were so cru-el-ly sow-ing the tares;
2. Sow-ing the tares, how dark the black sin, Mingling a curse with life's sweetest hymn, And heeding no an-guish, no pit-e-ous pray'rs, While we were so cru-el-ly sow-ing the tares;
3. Sow-ing the tares that bring sor-row down, Robs of its jew-els life's fair-est crown; And turning to sil-ver the once golden hairs, Grown whit-er and whit-er as we sowed the tares;
4. Sow-ing the tares un-der cov-er of night, Which might have been wheat, all golden and bright; O heart, turn to God with repentance and pray'r, And plead for for-give-ness for sow-ing the tares;

REFRAIN.

Sow-ing the tares, Sow-ing the tares, We plead for for-give-ness for sow-ing the tares.

55. Lead, Kindly Light.

LUX BENIGNA.

3 My Lord calls you—He calls you by the gospel;
  The trumpet sounds it to your soul,—
  You haint got long to stay here.
    Cho.—Steal away, etc.

4 Your wife's heart is breaking—poor children stand trembling;
  Oh take the words of comfort home,—
  For you haint got long to stay here.
    Cho.—Steal away, etc.

From "Jubilee Songs," by permission of BIGLOW & MAIN.

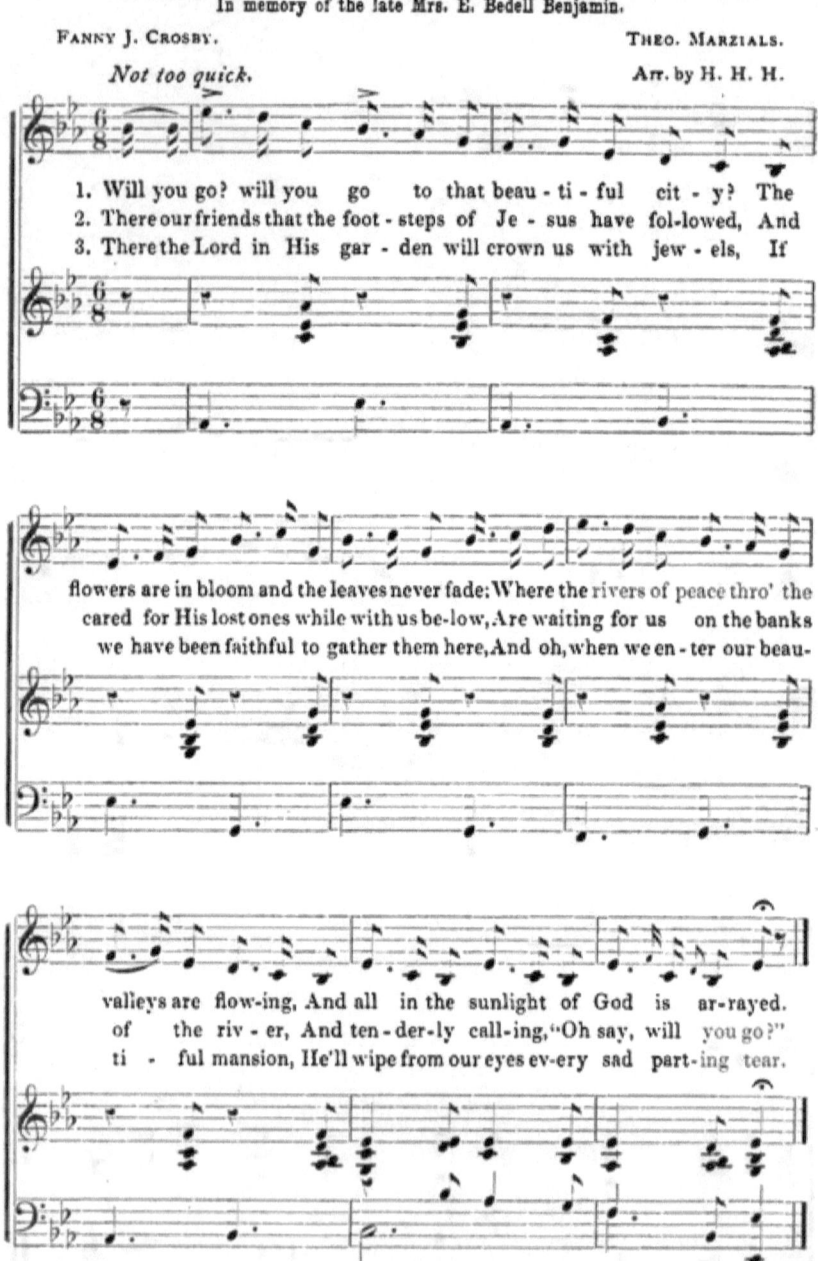

The Garden of Our Lord. Concluded.

She Is Coming Home To-morrow. Concluded.

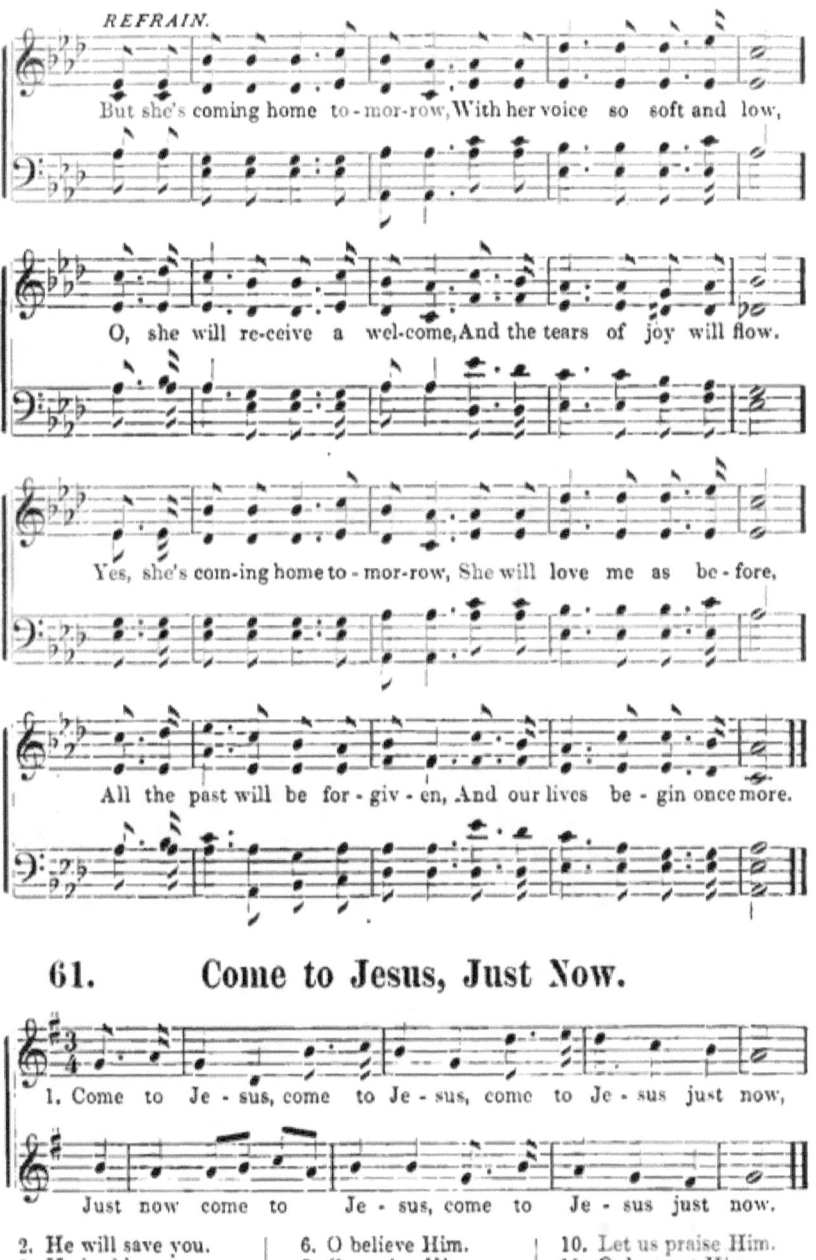

REFRAIN.

But she's coming home to-morrow, With her voice so soft and low,
O, she will receive a welcome, And the tears of joy will flow.
Yes, she's coming home to-morrow, She will love me as before,
All the past will be forgiven, And our lives begin once more.

61. Come to Jesus, Just Now.

1. Come to Jesus, come to Jesus, come to Jesus just now,
Just now come to Jesus, come to Jesus just now.

2. He will save you.
3. He is able.
4. He is willing.
5. He is waiting.
6. O believe Him.
7. O receive Him.
8. Jesus loves you.
9. He will bless you.
10. Let us praise Him.
11. Only trust Him.
12. I love Jesus.
13. Hallelujah, hallelujah.

62. Our Standard.

HENRY H. HADLEY.   WM. J. KIRKPATRICK, by per.

1. We all have a-greed on a stand-ard, That dai-ly we
2. As men of in-tel-li-gent wis-dom, Our thoughts on our
3. Our glass-es at lunch, if we take them, Our glass-es of
4. Yet I was a slave to the hab-it, It threatened my

mean to pur-sue, To drink when engaged at our la-bors, We've
du-ties should be, But drink makes them dull and in-ac-tive, A
wine or of beer, Will cloud both our rea-son and judgment, That
hopes and my all, They said, "Je-sus on-ly can save you," So with

CHORUS.

made up our minds will not do We've come to this con-clu-sion, By
truth that we plain-ly can see.
ought to be stead-y and clear.
His help I drink none at all.

which we mean to a-bide, We can't make a busi-ness of

drink-ing, And do oth-er busi-ness be-side. We

Copyright, 1890, by WM. J. KIRKPATRICK.

Our Standard. Concluded.

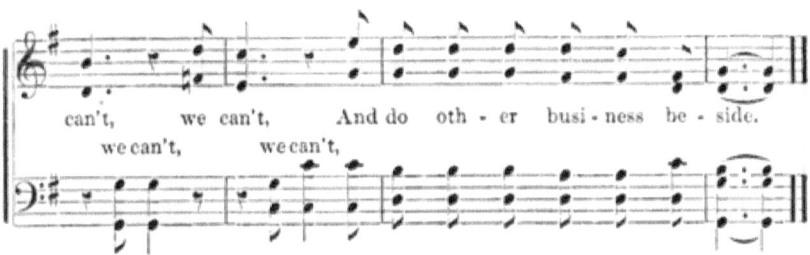

can't, we can't, And do oth-er busi-ness be-side.
we can't, we can't,

63. Now I Feel the Sacred Fire.

1. Now I feel the sa-cred fire, Kind-ling, flam-ing, glow-ing,
   High-er still and ris-ing higher, All my soul o'er-flow-ing;
2. Now I am from bondage freed, Ev-ery bond is riv-en;
   Je-sus makes me free in-deed, Just as free as heav-en:

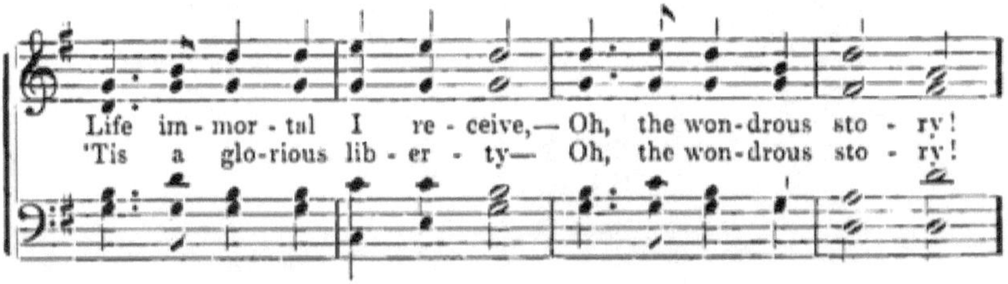

Life im-mor-tal I re-ceive,— Oh, the won-drous sto-ry!
'Tis a glo-rious lib-er-ty— Oh, the won-drous sto-ry!

I was dead, but now I live, Glo-ry! glo-ry! glo-ry!
I was bound, but now I'm free, Glo-ry! glo-ry! glo-ry!

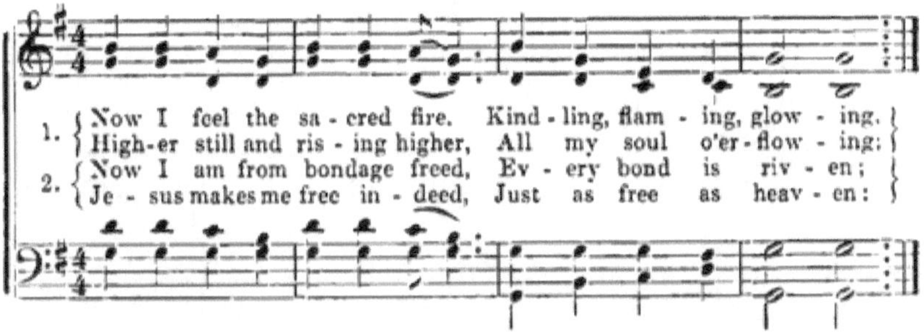

3 Let the testimony roll,
   Roll through every nation;
 Witnessing from soul to soul,
   This immense salvation,
 Now I know it's full and free;
   Oh, the wondrous story!
 For I feel it saving me,
   Glory! glory! glory!

4 Glory be to God on high,
   Glory be to Jesus!
 He hath brought salvation nigh,
   From all sin He frees us,
 Let the golden harp of God
   Ring the wondrous story;
 Let the pilgrim shout aloud
   Glory! glory! glory!

I'll Feed On Husks No More. *Concluded.*

Fa-ther's love im-plore, Con-fess my wrong: His par-don seek, His par-don seek, And feed on husks no more.

---

65. Art Thou Weary.

STEPHANOS.

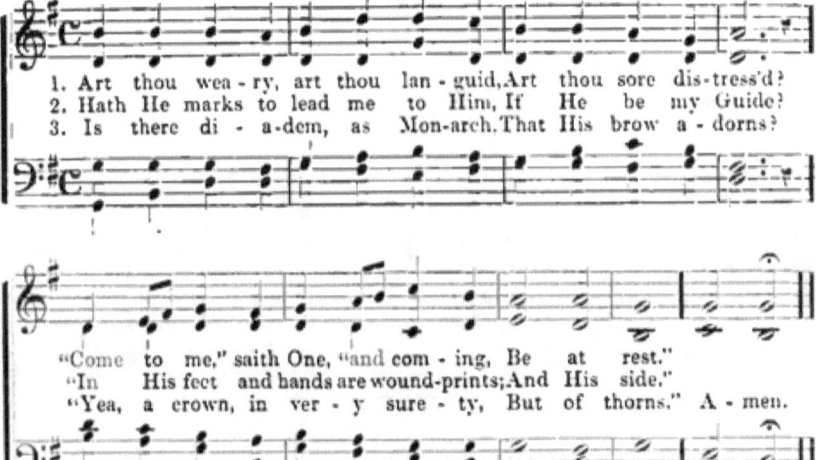

1. Art thou wea-ry, art thou lan-guid, Art thou sore dis-tress'd?
2. Hath He marks to lead me to Him, If He be my Guide?
3. Is there di-a-dem, as Mon-arch, That His brow a-dorns?

"Come to me," saith One, "and com-ing, Be at rest."
"In His feet and hands are wound-prints; And His side."
"Yea, a crown, in ver-y sure-ty, But of thorns." A-men.

4 If I find Him, if I follow,
   What His guerdon here?
"Many a sorrow, many a labor,
   Many a tear."

5 If I still hold closely to Him,
   What hath He at last?
"Sorrow vanquish'd, labor ended,
   Jordan pass'd."

6 If I ask Him to receive me,
   Will He say me nay?
"Not till earth, and not till heaven
   Pass away."

7 Finding, following, keeping, struggling,
   Is He sure to bless?
"Saints, apostles, prophets, martyrs,
   Answer, Yes."

66. Mount Calvary.

Dedicated to L. P. Tibbals.

For "Rescue Songs." Words and Music by D. C. WRIGHT.

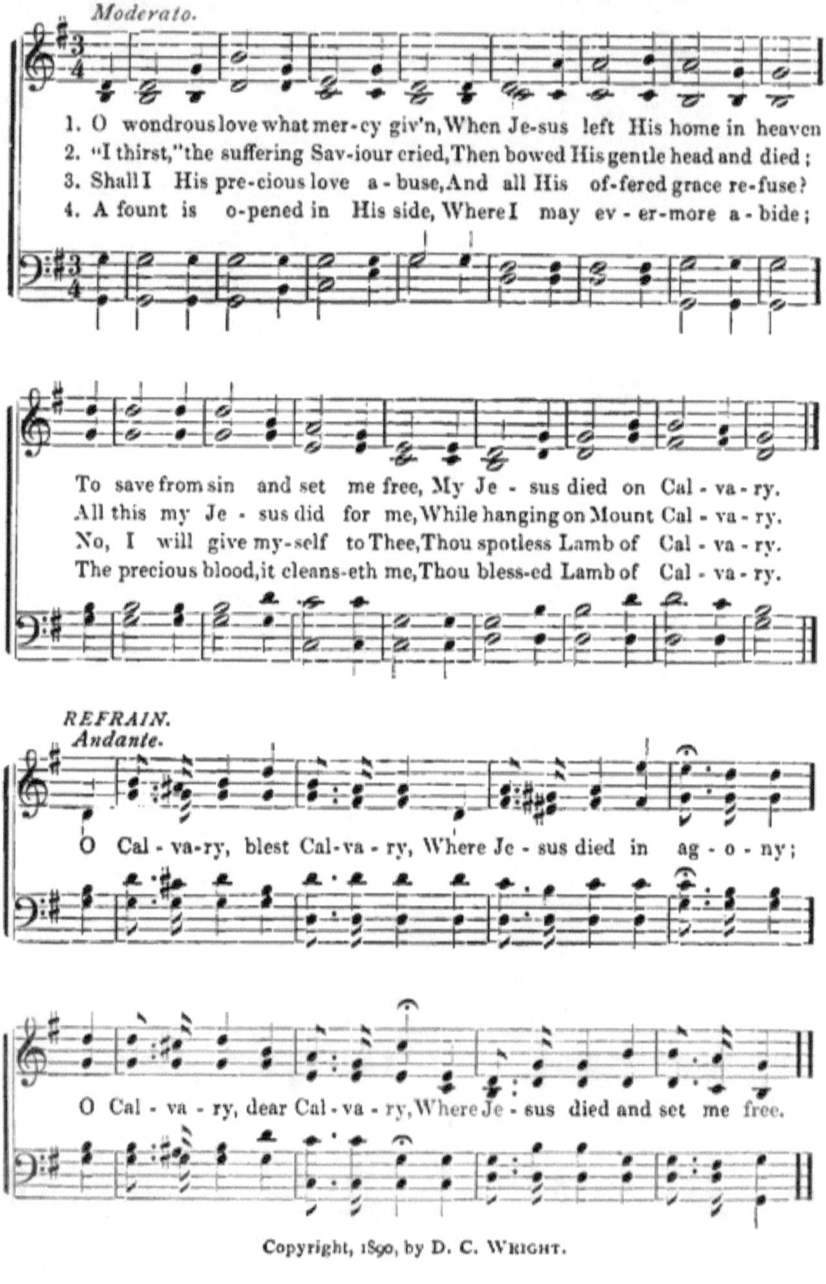

Moderato.

1. O wondrous love what mer-cy giv'n, When Je-sus left His home in heaven
2. "I thirst," the suffering Sav-iour cried, Then bowed His gentle head and died;
3. Shall I His pre-cious love a-buse, And all His of-fered grace re-fuse?
4. A fount is o-pened in His side, Where I may ev-er-more a-bide;

To save from sin and set me free, My Je-sus died on Cal-va-ry.
All this my Je-sus did for me, While hanging on Mount Cal-va-ry.
No, I will give my-self to Thee, Thou spotless Lamb of Cal-va-ry.
The precious blood, it cleans-eth me, Thou bless-ed Lamb of Cal-va-ry.

REFRAIN. Andante.

O Cal-va-ry, blest Cal-va-ry, Where Je-sus died in ag-o-ny;

O Cal-va-ry, dear Cal-va-ry, Where Je-sus died and set me free.

Copyright, 1890, by D. C. WRIGHT.

3 The brightest day that ever I saw,
   Coming for to carry me home,
  When Jesus washed my sins away,
   Coming for to carry me home.
    Swing low, etc.

4 I'm sometimes up and sometimes down,
   Coming for to carry me home,
  But still my soul feels heavenly bound,
   Coming for to carry me home.
    Swing low, etc.

From "Jubilee Songs," by permission of BIGLOW & MAIN.

69. For you and for me.

W. L. T. *Very Slow. pp* **Will L. Thompson.**

1. Soft-ly and tenderly Jesus is calling, Calling for you and for me;
2. Why should we tarry when Jesus is pleading, Pleading for you and for me?
3. Time is now fleeting, the moments are passing, Passing from you and from me;
4. Oh, for the wonderful love he has promis'd, Promis'd for you and for me,

See on the portals he's waiting and watching, Watching for you and for me.
Why should we linger and heed not his mercies, Mercies for you and for me.
Shadows are gath'ring, death beds are coming, Coming for you and for me.
Though we have sinn'd, he has mercy and pardon, Pardon for you and for me.

CHORUS.

Come home,.. Come home,.. Ye who are weary, come home...
  come home,   come home,

Earnestly, tenderly, Jesus is calling, Calling, O sinner, come home!

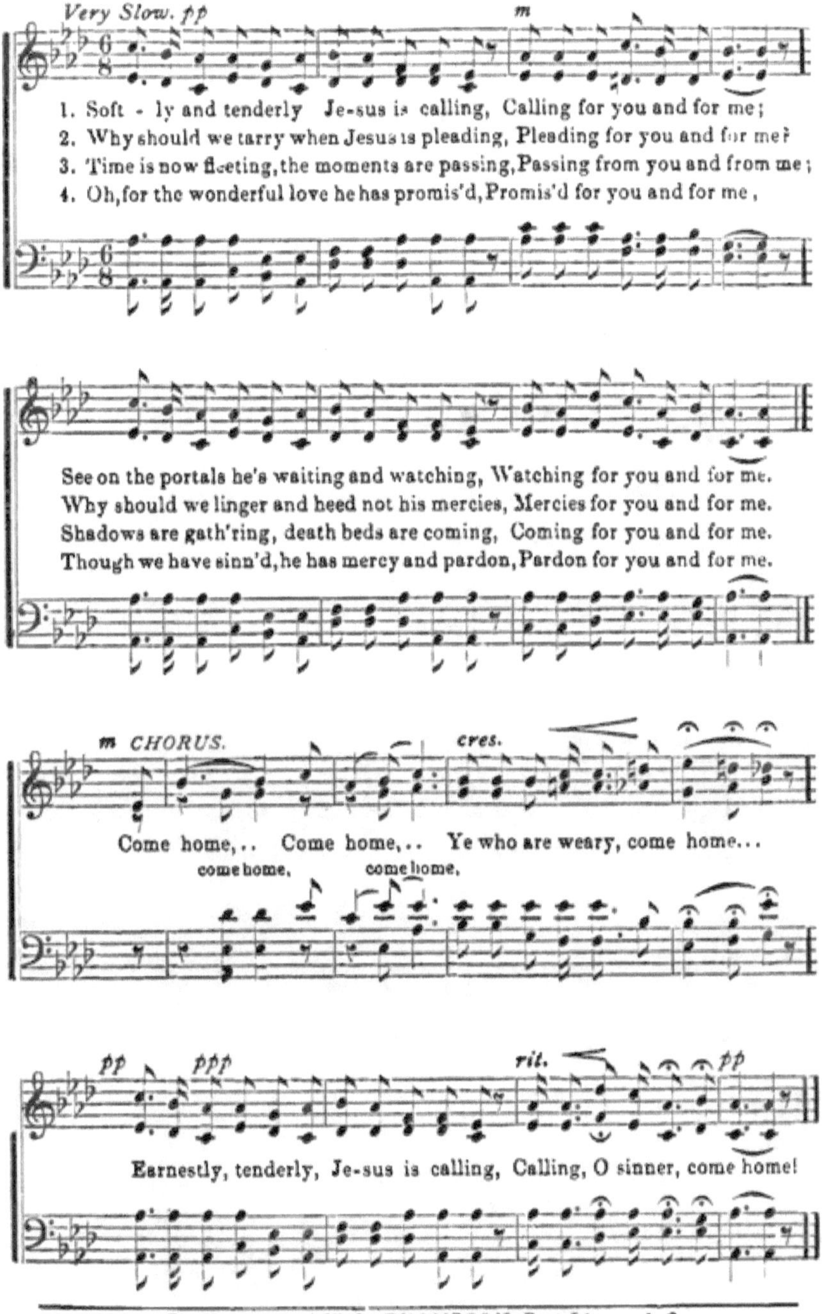

By permission of W. L. THOMPSON, East Liverpool, O.

Take the Whole Armour. Concluded.

ar-mour of God, That so ye may stand in the e - vil day.

71. Crown Him.

"Thou hast crowned him with glory and honor."

Rev. Thos. Kelly.   (Psalm 8: 5.)   Arr. by Geo. G. Stebbins. By per.

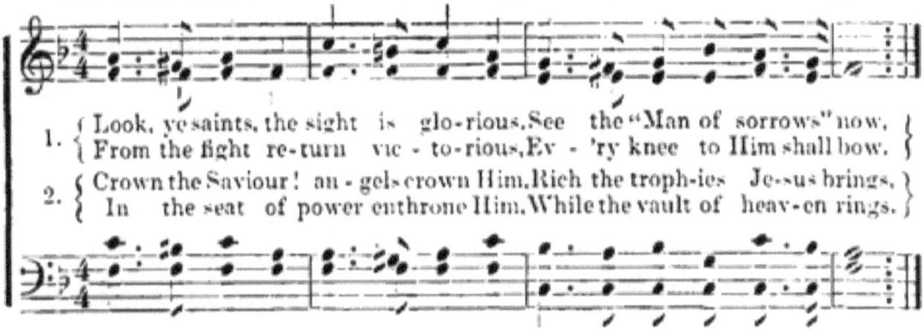

1. Look, ye saints, the sight is glo-rious, See the "Man of sorrows" now,
   From the fight re-turn vic - to-rious, Ev - 'ry knee to Him shall bow.
2. Crown the Saviour! an - gels crown Him, Rich the troph-ies Je-sus brings,
   In the seat of power enthrone Him, While the vault of heav-en rings.

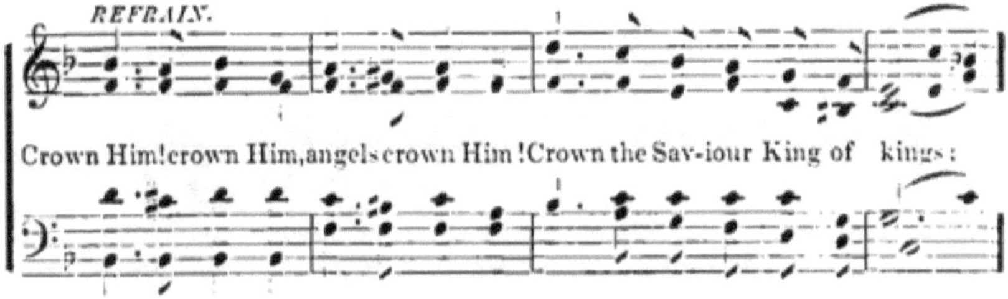

REFRAIN.

Crown Him! crown Him, angels crown Him! Crown the Sav-iour King of kings;

Crown Him! crown Him, an-gels crown Him! Crown the Saviour King of kings.

3 Sinners in derision crowned Him,
  Mocking thus the Saviour's claim,
  Saints and angels crowd around Him,
  Own His title, praise His name.

4 Hark! the bursts of acclamation!
  Hark! these loud, triumphant chords,
  Jesus takes the highest station,
  Oh, what joy the sight affords!

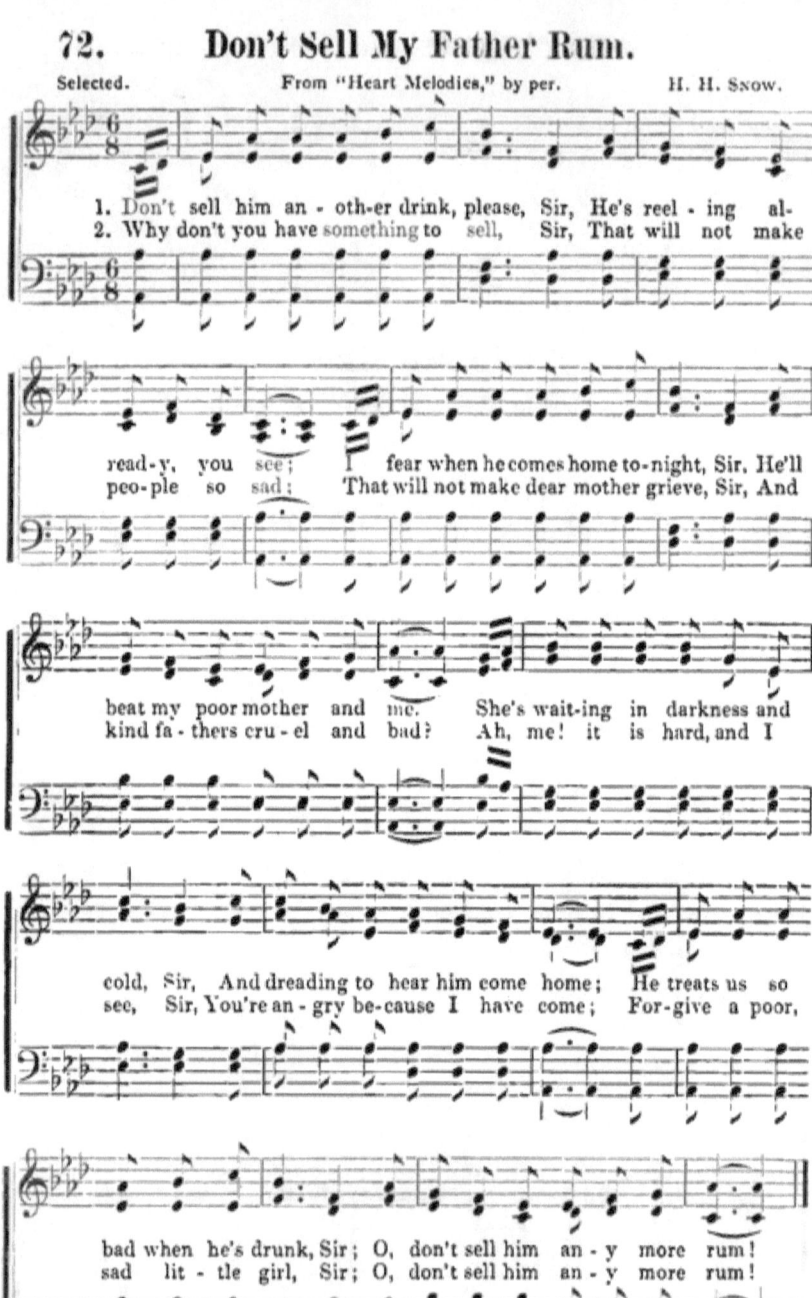

74. That Old, Old Story is True.

D. B. WATKINS. E. O. EXCELL.

1. There's a wonderful story I've heard long ago, 'Tis call'd "The sweet story of old;" I hear it so often, wherever I go, That same old story is told; And I've thought it was strange that so often they'd tell That story as if it were

2. They told of a being so lovely and pure, That came to the Earth to dwell, To seek for his lost ones, and make them secure From death and the power of hell; That he was despis'd, and with thorns he was crown'd, On the cross was extended to

3. He arose and ascended to heaven, we're told, Triumphant o'er death and hell; He's preparing a place in that city of gold, Where loved ones forever may dwell. Where our kindred we'll meet, and we'll nevermore part, And

4. O that wonderful story I love to repeat, Of peace and good will to men; There's no story to me that is half so sweet, As I hear it again and again. He invites you to come—he will freely receive, And this message he sendeth to

Copyright 1896 by E. O. EXCELL.

That Old, Old Story is True. Concluded.

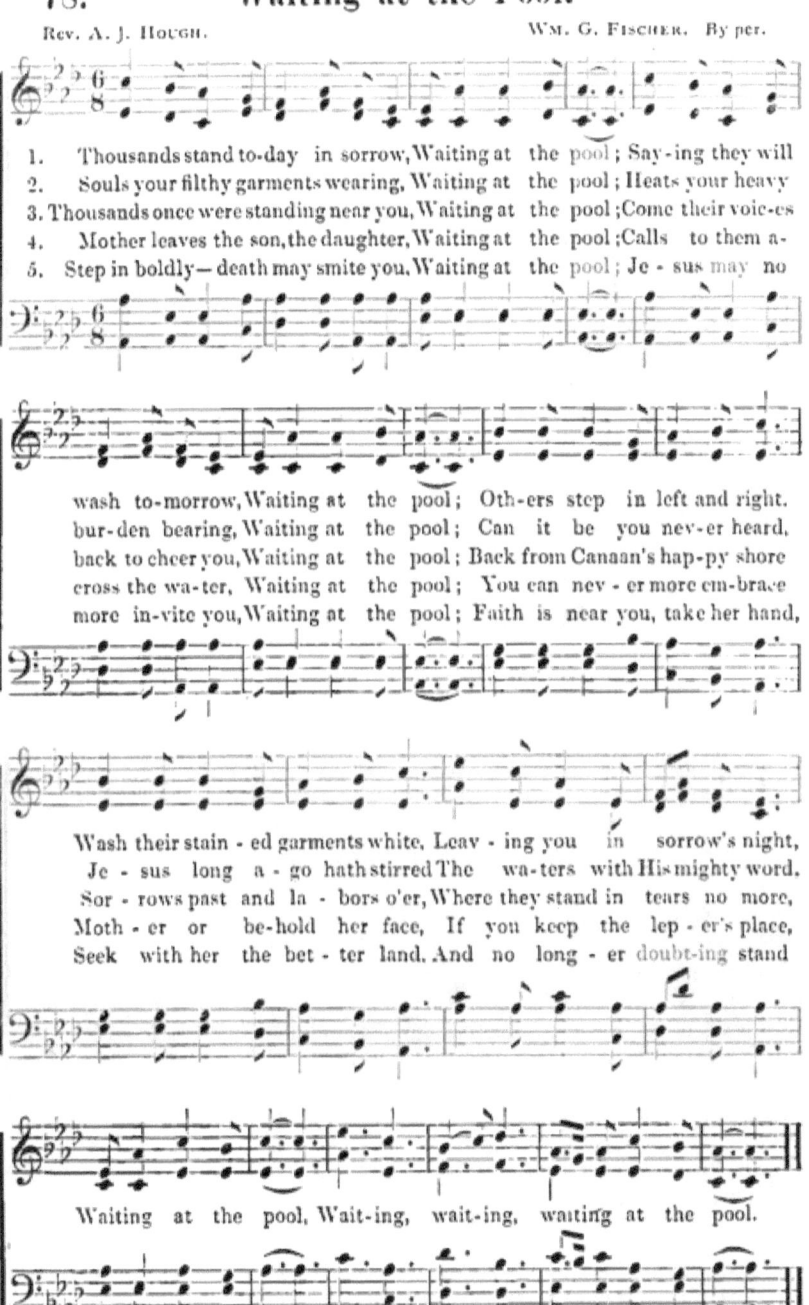

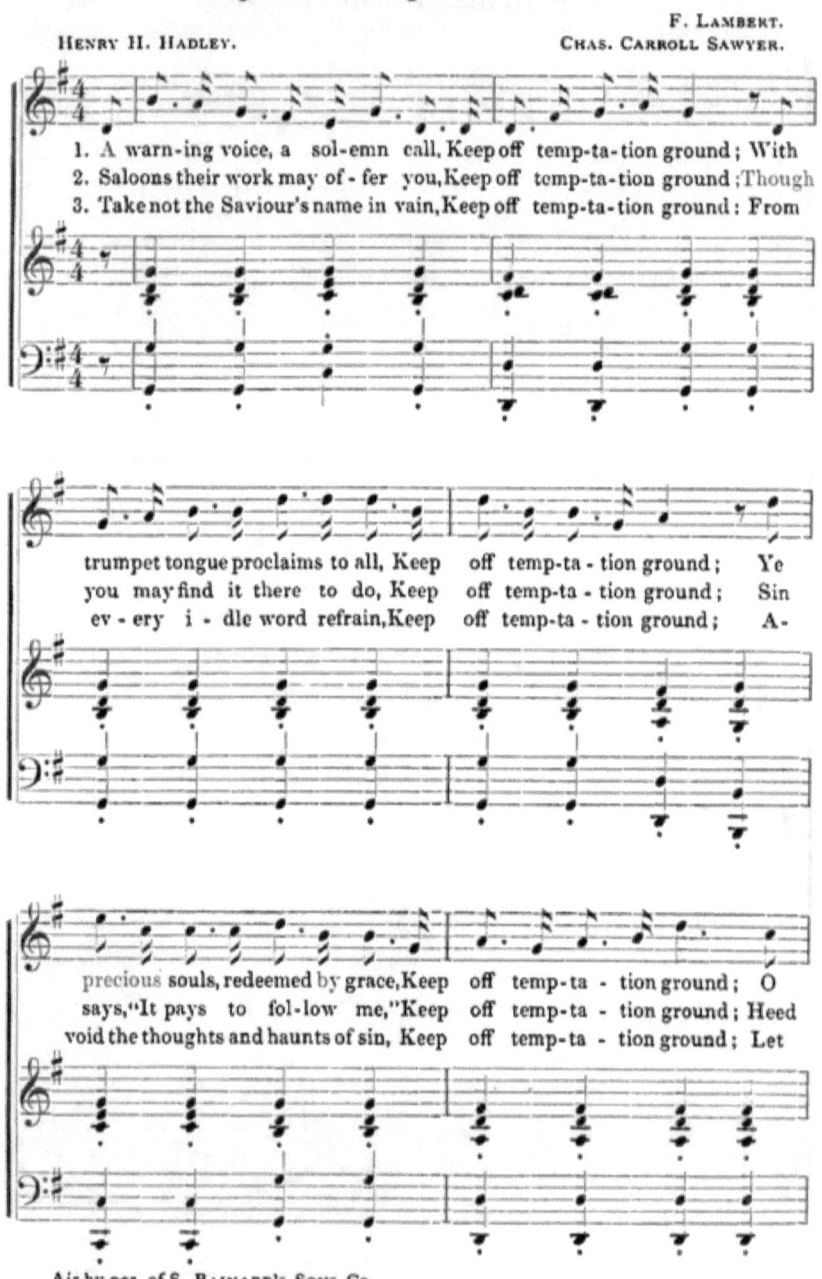

80. What's the News.

Words arranged by W. H. G. To Mrs. A. A. A. Rev. W. H. Gristweit.

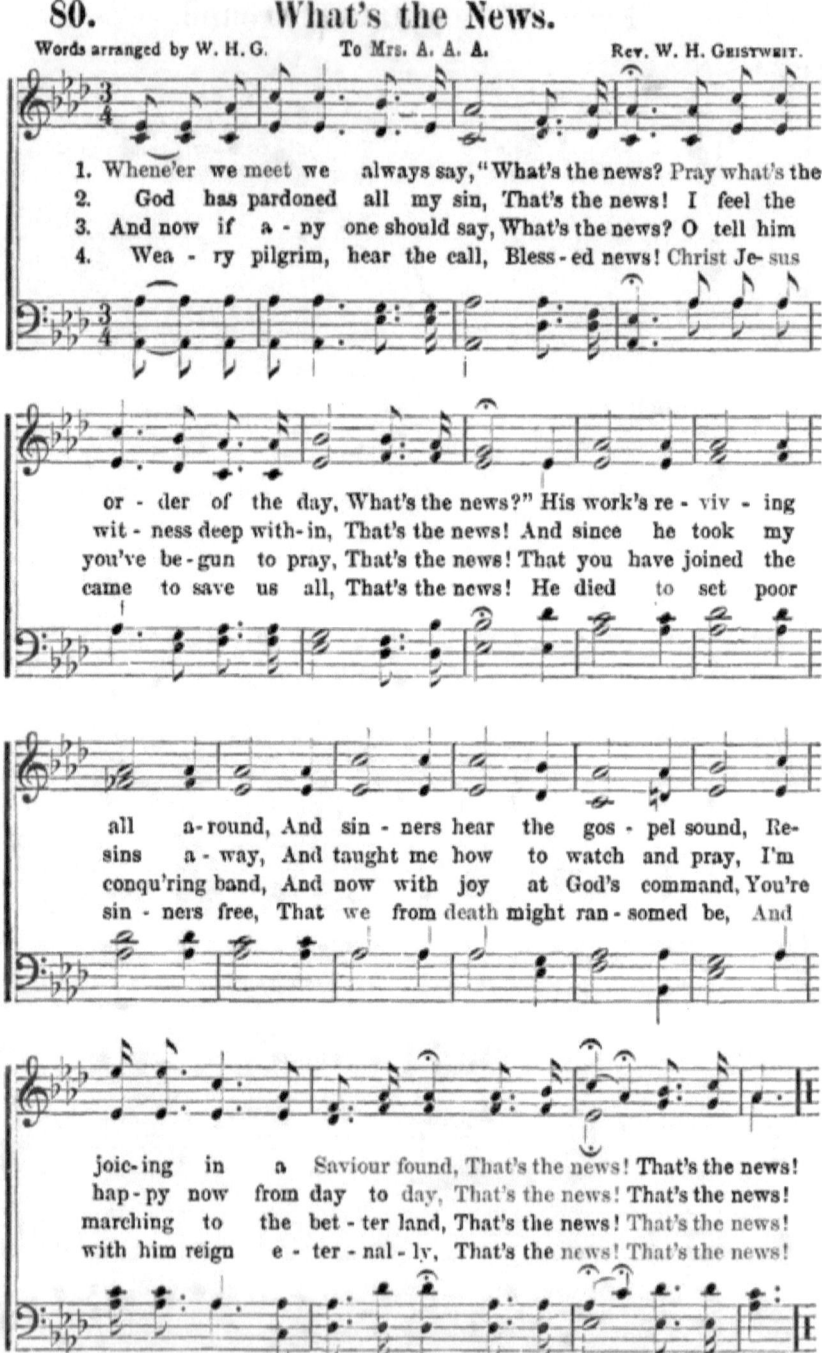

1. Whene'er we meet we always say, "What's the news? Pray what's the or-der of the day, What's the news?" His work's re-viv-ing all a-round, And sin-ners hear the gos-pel sound, Re-joic-ing in a Saviour found, That's the news! That's the news!
2. God has pardoned all my sin, That's the news! I feel the wit-ness deep with-in, That's the news! And since he took my sins a-way, And taught me how to watch and pray, I'm hap-py now from day to day, That's the news! That's the news!
3. And now if a-ny one should say, What's the news? O tell him you've be-gun to pray, That's the news! That you have joined the conqu'ring band, And now with joy at God's command, You're marching to the bet-ter land, That's the news! That's the news!
4. Wea-ry pilgrim, hear the call, Bless-ed news! Christ Je-sus came to save us all, That's the news! He died to set poor sin-ners free, That we from death might ran-somed be, And with him reign e-ter-nal-ly, That's the news! That's the news!

Copyright, 1895, by John J. Hood.

From TEMPLE THEMES AND SONGS, by per. J. J. Hood., Phila., Pa.

82. Willing Workers.

To the "willing worker" in the Rescue Volunteers of America.

IDA L. REED. W. A. OGDEN.

1. Onward, Rescue Volunteers, Who to God belong, Serve Him now with gladness, And with pray'r and song, For His love is faithful, and His promise true; In the world about us there is much to do.
2. Onward, Rescue Volunteers, Doing what we can For the Master's glory, Till He comes again. In His field we'll labor, in His cause we'll pray; Lead the lost to Jesus, on our pilgrim way.
3. Onward, Rescue Volunteers, Now and ever be What the Lord would have us, Serve Him faithfully; All our talents give Him for we are His own, Labor for His glory, and for His alone.

CHORUS.

Forward, workers, to your vows be true; Great the harvest, laborers are few! God hath called us, We His voice have heard, Go forward, workers for the Lord.

Copyright, 1890, by W. A. OGDEN.

83. "Try Him for Twenty-four Hours."

Henry H. Hadley. Arranged for "Rescue Songs."

1. Who will come to Christ the Lord? Who will trust His precious word?
2. Who will ask His aid divine? Who the fatal cup resign?

Who the armor on will gird?—"Only for a day?"
Who will say, "The Lord is mine?"—"Only for a day?"

Who for right will make a start? Who to Jesus give your heart?
Who from words profane will cease? Who will tread the path of peace?

Who will choose the better part?—"Try Him for a day?"
Who from sin will find release?—"Try Him for a day?"

3 Who will take the Saviour's hand?
Who will join our Royal band?
Who obey the Lord's command,
   "Only for a day?"
Who will view Him on the tree?
Who will say "He died for me"?
Who will take salvation free?—
   "Take it *now, to-day.*"

4 If where healing waters flow,
You His tender love could know,
You would *never* let Him go,—
   Never for a day.
If you now for Him decide:
In His mercy if you hide,
You will want no other guide—
   Never, for a day.

Copyright, 1890, by H. H. Hadley.

Backward, Turn Backward. Concluded.

mother, who taught me to say, "Father, forgive me the wrongs I have done, Father, forgive me thro' Jesus Thy Son."
take me a poor wretched slave? Mother still whispers that if I believe, Pardon thro' Jesus I yet may receive.
turning to Jesus the King." Mother will join in the song when she hears, "Saved is the boy that has wandered for years."

87. I'm Going Home to Die No More.

Wm. Hunter, D. D. Arranged for this work.

1. My heav'nly home is bright and fair; Nor pain, nor death can enter there:
Its glitt'ring tow'rs the sun outshine; That heav'nly mansion shall be mine.

Cho. I'm going home, I'm going home, I'm going home to die no more!
To die no more, to die no more; I'm going home to die no more!

2 My Father's house is built on high,
Far, far above the starry sky;
When from this earthly prison free,
That heavenly mansion mine shall be.

3 While here, a stranger far from home,
Affliction's waves may round me foam;
Although like Lazarus, sick and poor,
My heavenly mansion is secure.

4 Let others seek a home below,
Which flames devour, or waves o'erflow;
Be mine a happier lot to own
A heavenly mansion near the throne.

5 Then fail this earth, let stars decline,
And sun and moon refuse to shine,
All nature sink and cease to be,
That heavenly mansion stands for me.

Rescue Song. Concluded.

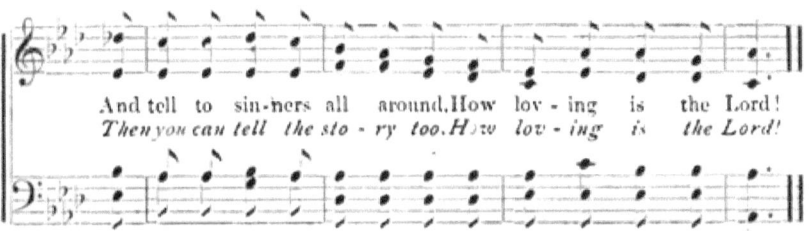

89. Glory to His Name.

E. A. Hoffman. By per.   Psa. 63: 4.   Rev. J. H. Stockton.

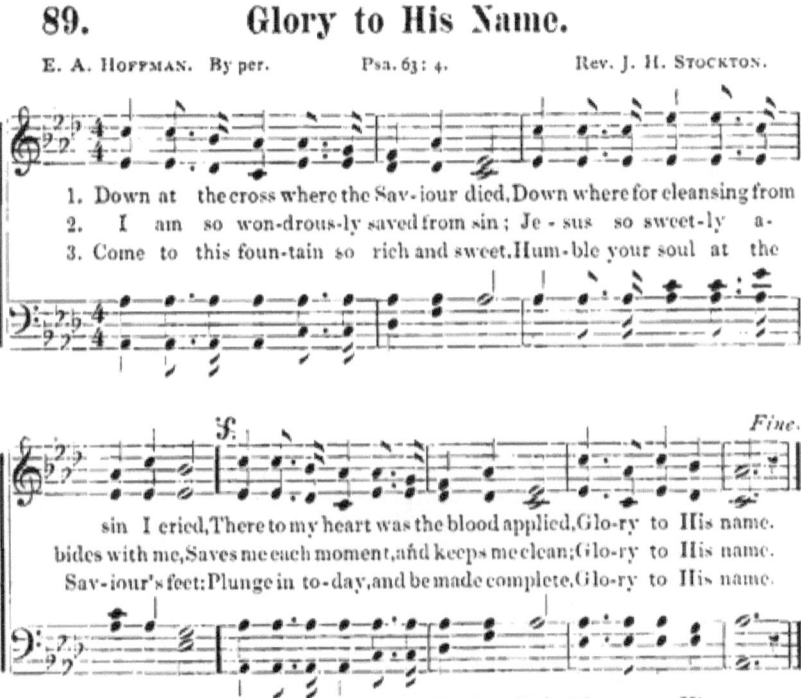

"Overcomers." Concluded.

born of God, Shall o-ver-come by the blood.
rai-ment white, That o-ver-comes by the blood.
tree of life, That o-ver-comes by the blood.
temple of God, That o-ver-comes by the blood.

CHORUS.

O, the precious, precious blood! O, the cleans-ing, heal-ing flood!
O, the pow'r and the love of God, Thro' the blood of the Lamb!

                           5
Rev. 3: 5.   ‖: What shall he hear? :‖ that overcometh
                By the blood of the Lamb?
                ‖: He shall hear his name con-|fessed in heaven, :‖
                That overcomes by the blood.

                           6
Rev. 21: 7.   ‖: What shall he have? :‖ that overcometh
                By the blood of the Lamb?
                ‖: God will give him all things, and|make him His son, :‖
                That overcomes by the blood.

                           7
Rev. 3: 21.   ‖: Where shall he sit? :‖ that overcometh
                By the blood of the Lamb?
                ‖: He shall sit with|Jesus, on His throne, :‖
                That overcomes by the blood.

                           8
1 John 5: 4.   ‖: What is the victory? :‖ that overcometh
                By the blood of the Lamb?
                ‖: Faith is the victory that|overcometh :‖
                By the blood of the Lamb.

The Sinner and the Song. (Concluded.)

4 Therefore whatsoe'er betideth,
  Night or day,
Know His love for thee provideth
  Good alway.
Crown of sorrows gladly taking,
For His sake all else forsaking,
Sweetly bending to His will,
  Patient—still.

5 To His own the Saviour giveth
    Daily strength;
  And to each heart that believeth,
    Joy at last.
  For the lambs the Shepherd careth,
  In His bosom them He beareth:
  While thus folded to His breast,
    They may rest.

Used by permission.

97. God's Promises.

Words by Mrs. Mary D. James. 2 Peter 1:4. Music by Wm. J. Kirkpatrick.

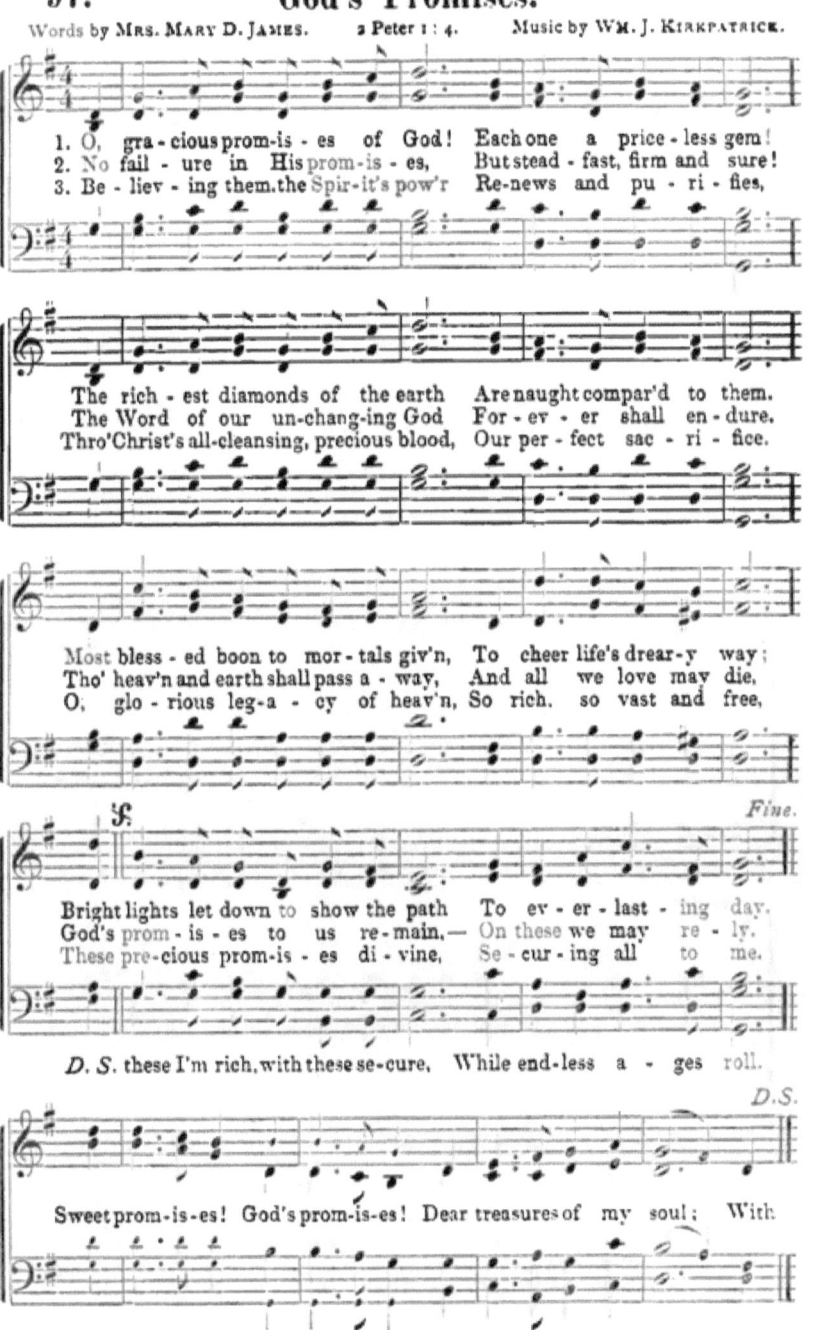

1. O, gracious promises of God! Each one a priceless gem! The richest diamonds of the earth Are naught compar'd to them. Most blessed boon to mortals giv'n, To cheer life's dreary way; Bright lights let down to show the path To everlasting day.
2. No failure in His promises, But steadfast, firm and sure! The Word of our unchanging God Forever shall endure. Tho' heav'n and earth shall pass away, And all we love may die, God's promises to us remain,— On these we may rely.
3. Believing them, the Spirit's pow'r Renews and purifies, Thro' Christ's all-cleansing, precious blood, Our perfect sacrifice. O, glorious legacy of heav'n, So rich, so vast and free, These precious promises divine, Securing all to me.

D.S. these I'm rich, with these secure, While endless ages roll.

Sweet promises! God's promises! Dear treasures of my soul; With

Copyright, 1885, by Wm. J. Kirkpatrick. Used by permission.

99. The Shepherd of The Sheep.

R. K. C.   R. Kelso Carter.

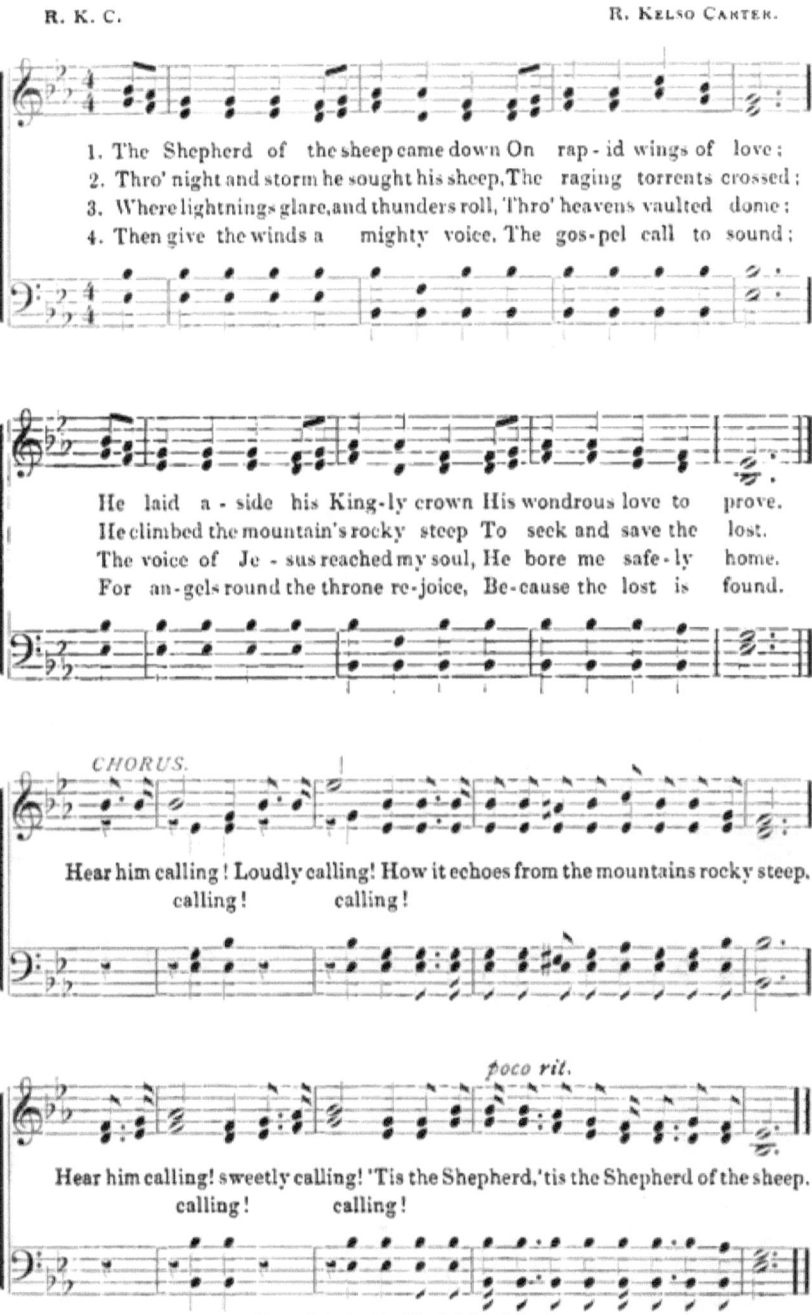

1. The Shepherd of the sheep came down On rap-id wings of love;
2. Thro' night and storm he sought his sheep, The raging torrents crossed;
3. Where lightnings glare, and thunders roll, Thro' heavens vaulted dome;
4. Then give the winds a mighty voice, The gos-pel call to sound;

He laid a-side his King-ly crown His wondrous love to prove.
He climbed the mountain's rocky steep To seek and save the lost.
The voice of Je-sus reached my soul, He bore me safe-ly home.
For an-gels round the throne re-joice, Be-cause the lost is found.

CHORUS.

Hear him calling! Loudly calling! How it echoes from the mountains rocky steep.
    calling!   calling!

poco rit.

Hear him calling! sweetly calling! 'Tis the Shepherd,'tis the Shepherd of the sheep.
    calling!   calling!

Copyright by R. K. CARTER, 1890.

100. I'll Bear It, Lord, For Thee.

FANNY J. CROSBY.   WM. J. KIRKPATRICK.

Suggested by the personal testimony of H. H. HADLEY, who was converted July 28, 1886, at the old Jerry McAuley Water St. Mission.

1. I longed to be a child of God, And do my Sav-iour's will;
And yet the sin that most I feared, I knew un-con-quered still.
"Dear Lord," I said,—for as I knelt I saw Him on the tree—
"This heav-y bur-den on my heart, I'll glad-ly bear for thee."

2. The cloud was lift-ed from my soul, My bur-den rolled a-way;
The light of joy a-round me shed, A calm and heavenly ray.
"Dear Lord," I said, "I praise thy name For thy rich grace to me;
My load is gone and now I rest, In per-pect peace with thee."

3. I heard a gen-tle voice with-in— A whis-per soft and mild;
"Thy sin was can-celled by His blood, Who owns thee for His child."
"Dear Lord," I said, "the work is thine, And thine the glo-ry be,
My life, my soul, my ev-ery pow'r, I con-se-crate to thee."

CHORUS.

So now for Him who died for me, I'm will-ing all to bear;

By permission.   Copyright, 1890, by WM. J. KIRKPATRICK.

102. Shall We Meet.

In Memory of Jane Riddel; Wm. H. (2); Lucy Hopkins; Little Lizzie, Lillie and other loved ones.
H. L. HASTINGS.   ELISHA S. RICE.

1. Shall we meet be-yond the riv-er, Where the sur-ges cease to roll?
2. Shall we meet in that blest harbor, When our storm-y voy-age's o'er?

Where, in all the bright for-ev-er, Sor-row ne'er shall press the soul?
Shall we meet and cast the an-chor, By the fair, ce-les-tial shore?

D.S.—Shall we meet be-yond the riv-er, Where the sur-ges cease to roll?

CHORUS.

Shall we meet, shall we meet, Shall we meet beyond the riv-er?

3 Shall we meet in yonder city,
   Where the towers of crystal shine?
  Where the walls are all of Jasper,
   Built by workmanship divine?

4 Where the music of the ransomed
   Rolls its harmony around,
  And creation swells the chorus
   With its sweet melodious sound.

5 Shall we meet there many a loved one,
   That was torn from our embrace?
  Shall we listen to their voices,
   And behold them face to face?

6 Shall we meet with Christ our Saviour,
   When he comes to claim his own?
  Shall we know His blessed favor,
   And sit down upon His throne?

103. The Child of a King.

1 My Father is rich in houses and lands,
He holdeth the wealth of the world in His hands!
Of rubies and diamonds, of silver and gold
His coffers are full,—he has riches untold.

CHO.—I'm the child of a King,
    The child of a King:
   With Jesus my Saviour
    I'm the child of a king.

2 My Father's own Son, who saves us from sin, [of men,
Once wandered o'er earth as the poorest
But now He is reigning forever on high,
And will give me a home in heaven by and by.

3 I once was an outcast stranger on earth,
A sinner by choice, an alien by birth!
But I've been adopted, my name's writ-ten down,—
An heir to a mansion, a robe, and a crown.

4 A tent or a cottage, why should I care?
They're building a palace for me over there! [sing:
Though exiled from home, yet, still I may
All glory to God; I'm the child of a King

104. Ring the Bells.

S. W. M.
S. Wesley Martin, by per.

106. There is a Time.

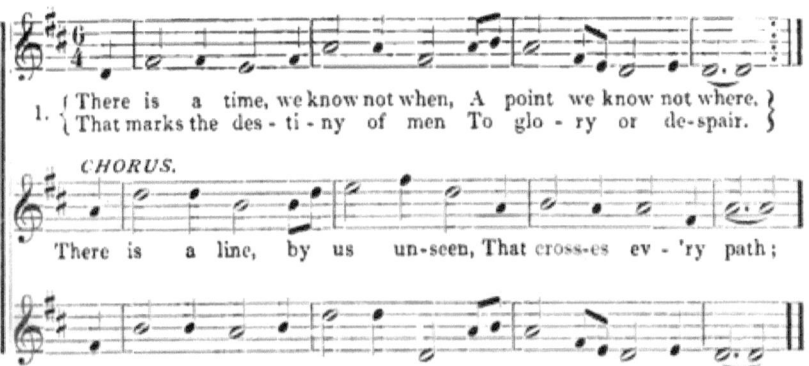

1. { There is a time, we know not when, A point we know not where,
   { That marks the des-ti-ny of men To glo-ry or de-spair.

CHORUS.

There is a line, by us un-seen, That cross-es ev-'ry path; The hid-den boun-da-ry be-tween God's pa-tience and His wrath.

107. The First Psalm.

Sing to the Tune above.

1 How blest is he, who ne'er consents
　　By ill advice to walk,
　Nor stands in sinner's ways, nor sits
　　Where men profanely talk;

2 But makes the perfect law of God,
　　His business and delight;
　Devoutly reads therein by day,
　　And meditates by night.

3 Like some fair tree, which, fed by streams,
　　With timely fruit does bend;
　He still shall flourish, and success
　　All his designs attend.

4 Ungodly men and their attempts,
　　No lasting root shall find;
　Untimely, blasted and dispersed,
　　Like chaff before the wind.

5 Their guilt shall strike the wicked dumb
　　Before their Judge's face;
　No formal hypocrite shall then
　　Among the saints have place.

6 For God approves the just men's ways;
　　To happiness they tend;
　But sinners and the paths they tread,
　　Shall both in ruin end.

5 Ho! all ye heavy-laden, come!
    Here's pardon, comfort, rest, and home;
    Ye wanderers from a Father's face,
    Return, accept His proffered grace.
    Ye tempted one, there's refuge nigh,
    "Jesus of Nazareth passeth by."

6 But if you still this call refuse,
    And all His wondrous love abuse,
    Soon will He sadly from you turn,
    Your bitter prayer for pardon spurn.
    "Too late! too late!" will be the cry—
    "Jesus of Nazareth *has passed by*."

109. I Can, I Will, I Do Believe.

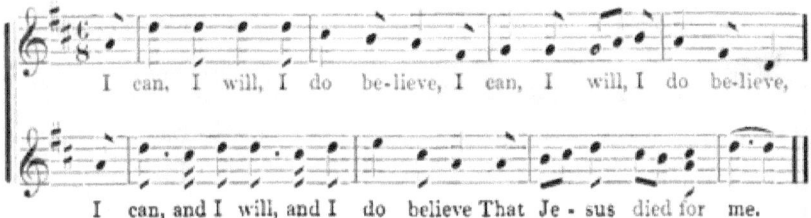

I can, I will, I do be-lieve, I can, I will, I do be-lieve,
I can, and I will, and I do believe That Je-sus died for me.

110. The Best of Books.

"First Hymn."

Arr. for "Rescue Songs." TUNE.—"Coronation."

1 Great God, with wonder and with praise,
  On all Thy works I look:
But still Thy wisdom, power, and grace,
  Shine brightest in Thy Book.

2 The stars that in their courses roll,
  Have much instruction given;
But Thy good Word informs my soul,
  How I may soar to heaven.

3 The fields provide me food, and show
  The goodness of the Lord;
But fruits of life and glory grow
  In Thy most Holy Word.

4 Here are my choicest treasures hid,
  Here my best comfort lies;
Here my desires are satisfied,
  And here my hopes arise.

5 Lord, make me understand Thy law;
  Show what my faults have been;
And from Thy gospel let me draw,
  Pardon for all my sin.

6 Here would I learn how Christ has died,
  To save my soul from hell;
Not all the books on earth besides,
  Such heavenly wonders tell.

7 Then let me love my Bible more,
  And take a fresh delight.
By day to read those wonders o'er,
  And meditate by night.

The King's Son. <small>Concluded.</small>

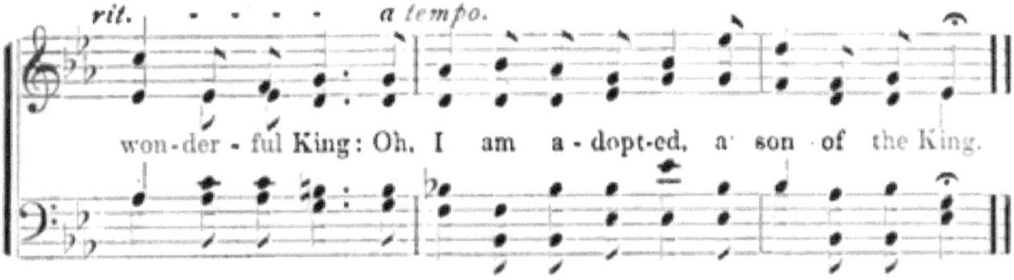

won-der-ful King: Oh, I am a-dopt-ed, a son of the King.

112. Gather Them In.

F. J. Van Alstyne.   Geo. C. Stebbins, by per.

1. Gather them in! for yet there is room At the feast that the King has spread;
2. Gather them in! for yet there is room; But our hearts—how they throb with pain,
3. Gather them in! for yet there is room;'Tis a message from God a-bove;

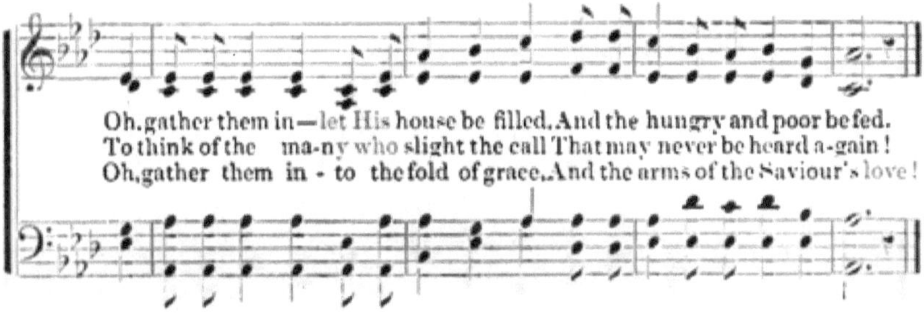

Oh, gather them in—let His house be filled, And the hungry and poor be fed.
To think of the ma-ny who slight the call That may never be heard a-gain!
Oh, gather them in - to the fold of grace, And the arms of the Saviour's love!

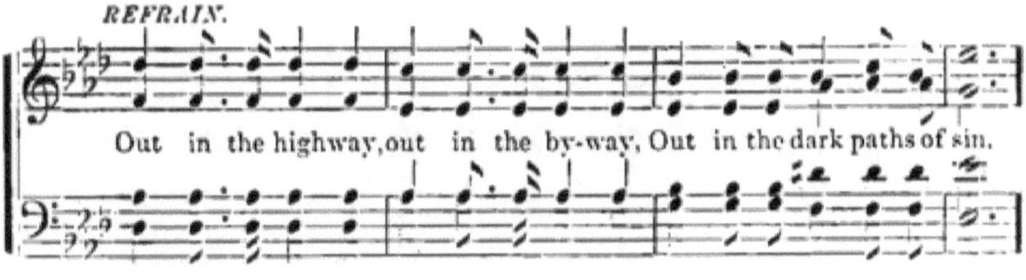

REFRAIN.

Out in the highway, out in the by-way, Out in the dark paths of sin,

Go forth, go forth, with a lov-ing heart, And gather the wand'rers in!

<small>Copyright, 1883, by Geo. C. Stebbins.</small>

114. Oh! the Lamb.

Chorus.—Oh! the Lamb, the lov-ing Lamb, The Lamb of Cal-va-ry! The Lamb that was slain. Yet lives a-gain, To in-ter-cede for me.

114½ Look Not on the Rosy Wine.

Rev. Frank Bottome, D. D.   Air.—"Auld Lang Syne."

1 O look not on the rosy wine,
    Touch not the sparkling bowl;
The honied sweetness to the lips
    Is poison to the soul.

2 O look not on the feath'ry foam
    That crowns the tankard's brim;
The symbol of the drunkard's home,
    The sign of death to him.

3 O look not on the oily slime,
    So quiet in the cup;
There lurks the hidden seeds of sin,
    And hell to those who sup.

4 O look not on the treacherous smile
    That lures thee to the spot
Where vice's skillful arts beguile
    And virtue is forgot.

5 O look not on the open hand
    That offers bribe or bait;
Behind the invitation bland
    The crowns of sin await.

6 O look not on the lurid glare
    That tempts unwary feet;
The laugh and wailing of despair
    Across the threshold meet.

7 O look not, taste not, handle not,
    Escape the fatal snare;
There's safety in the way of life,
    And only safety there!

115. The Old Time Religion.

Southern Song and Melody.

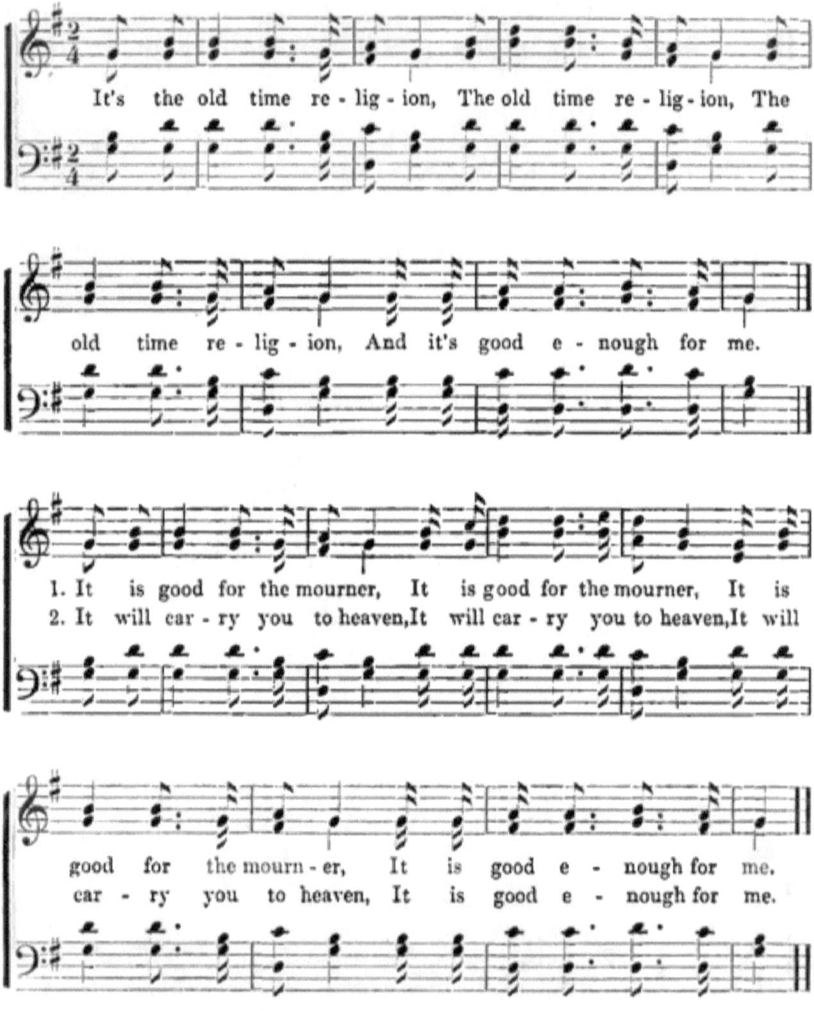

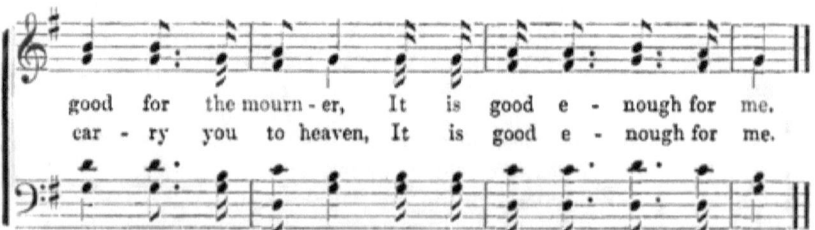

It's the old time re-lig-ion, The old time re-lig-ion, The old time re-lig-ion, And it's good e-nough for me.

1. It is good for the mourner, It is good for the mourner, It is good for the mourn-er, It is good e-nough for me.
2. It will car-ry you to heaven, It will car-ry you to heaven, It will car-ry you to heaven, It is good e-nough for me.

3 It brought me out of bondage, etc.
   Cho.—It's the old time religion, etc.

4 It is good when you are in trouble, etc.
   Cho.—It's the old time religion, etc.

5 It was good enough for Daniel, etc.
   Cho.—It's the old time religion, etc.

6 It was good enough for mother, etc.
   Cho.—It's the old time religion, etc.

7 It made me leave off drinking, etc.
   Cho.—It's the old time religion, etc.

8 It is good when you are dying, etc.
   Cho.—It's the old time religion, etc.

From "Jubilee Songs," by permission of BIGLOW & MAIN.

116. Jesus Took Me By the Hand.

"Jesus took him by the hand, and lifted him up."—MARK 9: 27.

ALICE M. LOWE. R. S. ROBSON, by per.

1. When my weary feet had wander'd, Far from God in paths of sin; And my fee-ble heart was crushing, 'Neath the weight of guilt with-in. To the world I looked for comfort, For I knew not where to fly; But a voice then sweetly whisper'd, Jesus now is pass-ing by.

2. In my help-less-ness I murmured, Lord, have mercy on my soul; Break these chains of sin that bind me, Make my wounded spir-it whole. Then in love He smiled upon me, Bade me lean up-on His breast; Saying, child, thou art for-giv-en, Freely will I give thee rest.

3. In the pres-ence of my Saviour, Sweetly resting at His feet; Sheltered from each storm and dan-ger, Here I find my joy com-plete. All my grief is chang'd to gladness, All my pain to pure delight; With my hand in His He guides me, Making all my pathway bright.

CHORUS.

Je-sus took me by the hand, Though my heart was full of sin; Wash'd me in His pre-cious blood, Made me snow-y white with-in.

Copyright, 1890, by R. S. ROBSON.

120. My Telegram's Gone.

JAS. M. SAWYER. By per.

1 What wondrous methods God has given!
Salvation wires from earth to heaven;
The Spirit's currents run up there:
I'll send a telegram of prayer.

CHO.—My telegram's gone, my telegram's gone,
To the palace of glory, my telegram's gone,
My Father's there; He'll answer prayer:
My telegram's gone, my telegram's gone.

2 His telegram is strong and free,
My message goes without a fee;
His office is the one I choose,
His promise is the form I use.

3 I wire for Him my soul to fill,
I wire for power to do His will;
I wire before the throne of grace,
I wire to reach the holy place.

4 I wire to get the Spirit's shower,
I wire for full salvation power;
For rescue from a drunkard's grave:
I wire for Him to come and save.

121. Glorious Morning.

J. BAKER.

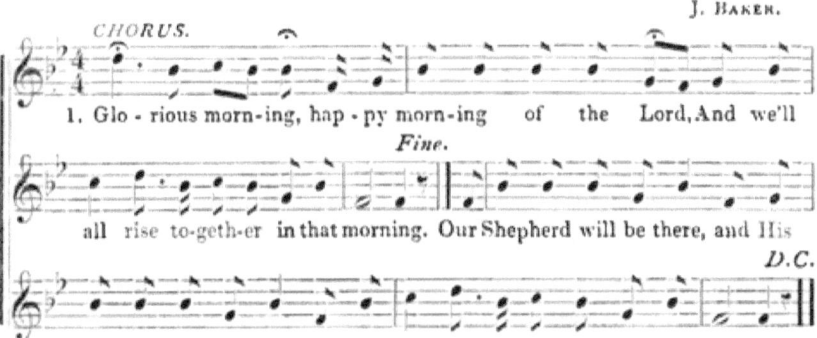

1. Glorious morning, happy morning of the Lord, And we'll all rise together in that morning. Our Shepherd will be there, and His sheep will all be there, And they'll all rise together in that morning.

2 Our converts will be there,
And their leader will be there.

3 Father Abra'm will be there,
And our children will be there.

4 Our fathers will be there,
And our mothers will be there.

5 Good old Moses will be there,
And brave Daniel will be there.

122. My Beautiful Home.

1 Above the waves of earthly strife,
Above the ills and cares of life,
Where all is peaceful, bright and fair,
My home is there, my home is there.

CHORUS.

My beautiful home, my beautiful home,
In the land where the glorified ever shall roam,
Where angels bright wear crowns of light,
My home is there, my home is there.

2 Away from sorrow, doubt and pain,
Away from worldly loss and gain,
From all temptations, tears and care,
My home is there, my home is there.

3 Where living fountains sweetly flow,
Where buds and flowers immortal grow,
Where trees their fruits celestial bear,
My home is there, my home is there.

4 Beyond the bright and pearly gates,
Where Jesus, loving Saviour, waits,
Where all is peaceful, bright and fair,
My home is there, my home is there.

123. Tell it to Jesus Alone.

"Tell it to Jesus."—Matt. 14: 12.

J. E. Rankin, D. D.
Rev. E. S. Lorenz. By per.

1. Are you wea-ry, are you heav-y-heart-ed? Tell it to Je-sus,
2. Do the tears flow down your cheeks un-bid-den? Tell it to Je-sus,
3. Do you fear the gath'ring clouds of sor-row? Tell it to Je-sus,
4. Are you troubled at the thought of dy-ing, Tell it to Je-sus,

Tell it to Je-sus; Are you griev-ing o-ver joys de-part-ed?
Tell it to Je-sus; Have you sins that to man's eye are hid-den?
Tell it to Je-sus; Are you anx-ious what shall be to-mor-row?
Tell it to Je-sus; For Christ's com-ing Kingdom are you sigh-ing?

CHORUS.

Tell it to Je-sus a-lone. Tell it to Je-sus, Tell it to Je-sus,
He is a friend that's well known: You have no oth-er
such a friend or broth-er? Tell it to Je-sus a-lone.

Copyright, 1880, by E. S. Lorenz.

124. The Waters of Jordan may Roll.

Words and Music by BALLINGTON BOOTH.—Used by permission.

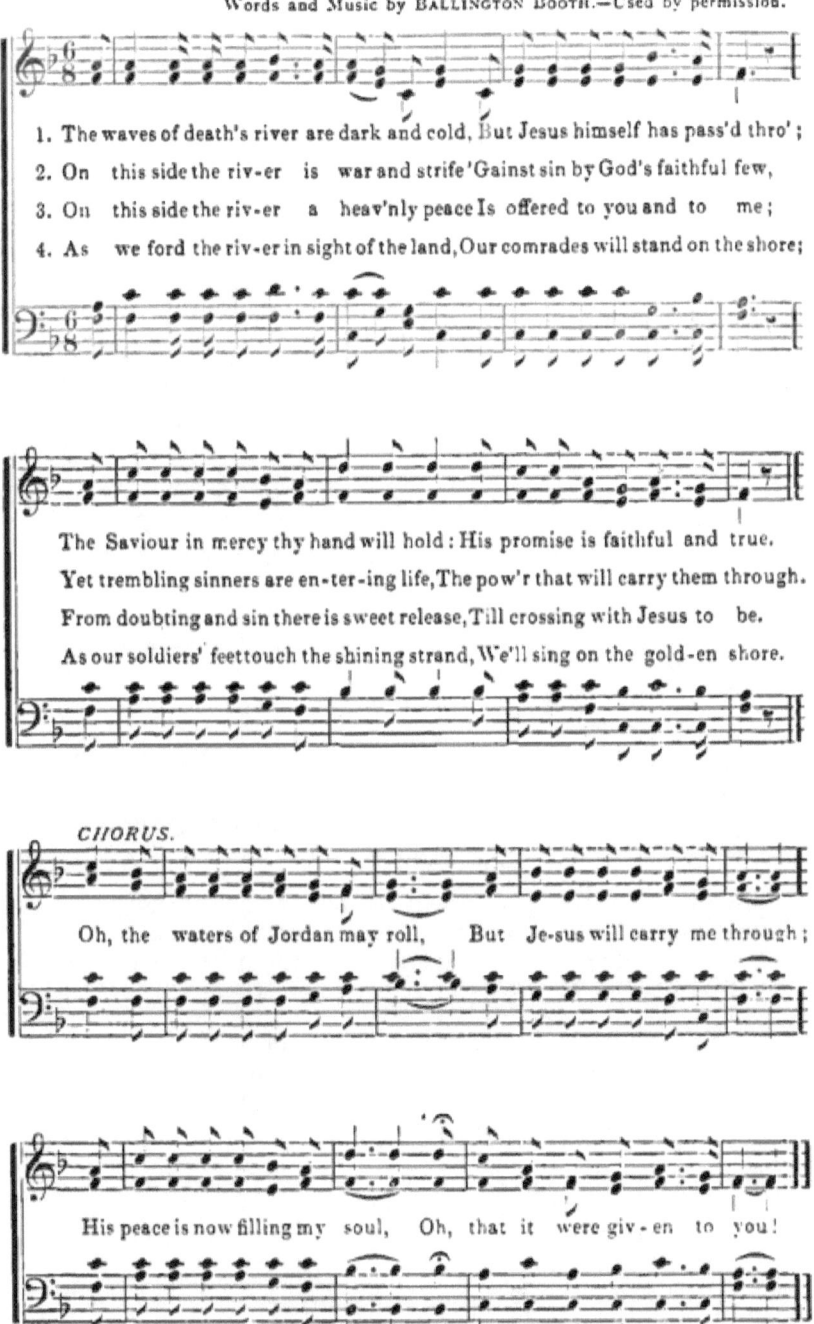

1. The waves of death's river are dark and cold, But Jesus himself has pass'd thro';
2. On this side the riv-er is war and strife 'Gainst sin by God's faithful few,
3. On this side the riv-er a heav'nly peace Is offered to you and to me;
4. As we ford the riv-er in sight of the land, Our comrades will stand on the shore;

The Saviour in mercy thy hand will hold: His promise is faithful and true.
Yet trembling sinners are en-ter-ing life, The pow'r that will carry them through.
From doubting and sin there is sweet release, Till crossing with Jesus to be.
As our soldiers' feet touch the shining strand, We'll sing on the gold-en shore.

CHORUS.

Oh, the waters of Jordan may roll, But Je-sus will carry me through;

His peace is now filling my soul, Oh, that it were giv-en to you!

125. A Mighty League of Prayer.

Dedicated to the "Grand Army of the Redeemed."

Words by Rev. F. Bottome, D. D.

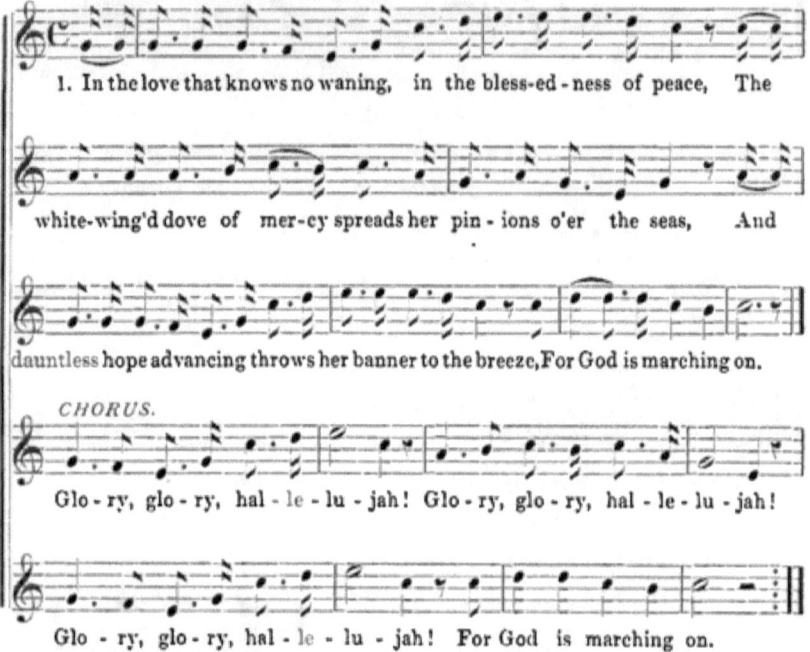

1. In the love that knows no waning, in the bless-ed-ness of peace, The white-wing'd dove of mer-cy spreads her pin-ions o'er the seas, And dauntless hope advancing throws her banner to the breeze, For God is marching on.

CHORUS.

Glo-ry, glo-ry, hal-le-lu-jah! Glo-ry, glo-ry, hal-le-lu-jah! Glo-ry, glo-ry, hal-le-lu-jah! For God is marching on.

2 Oh! by the widow's groaning, and the orphan's bitter tear,
And the tide of desolation that blighteth everywhere,
In the name of God we stand as one—a mighty league of prayer!
For God is marching on.—Cho.

3 We bring no hatred in our souls, no fetters in our hands,
But in the all-resistless power that only love commands;
We lift our eyes, and wait to see what faith in God demands,
For God is marching on.—Cho.

4 In vain the spoiler, band in hand, in proud defiance calls,
We answer back his hate with peace, and march around his walls,
Till, at the trumpet-blast of God, the mighty fortress falls,
For God is marching on.—Cho.

5 Then shout the tidings glorious—a glad and tireless band,
A league of faith to sweep away this evil from the land;
Hear the thunders of our legions rolling back from strand to strand,
For God is marching on.—Cho.

Copyright, 1890, by H. H. Hadley.

126. Trust Me.

CARRIE C. COE.
SPENCER W. COE.
May be sung in two sharps.

1. Lost and helpless, Jesus found me, Loved me sunk in guilt and sin; O-pened wide the door of mer-cy, Sweetly beck-on'd me, "Come in." Tempt-ed, sick, de-spised, and hope-less, Cast thy ev-'ry care on me, Bruis-ed, foot-sore, weak with wand'ring, Trust me, I will car - - ry thee.

2. Come to me for ev-'ry bless-ing, Come to me for help and rest, On-ly come thy need con-fess-ing, Come and lean up-on my breast. Oh, that voice, so sweet, so ten-der, Ri-v'ling rich-est mel-o-dy, Lov-ing-kind-ness, match-less, prec-ious,............... Loving-kindness rescued me.

Copyright, 1887, by SPENCER W. COE. By per.

127. There is a Green Hill Far Away.

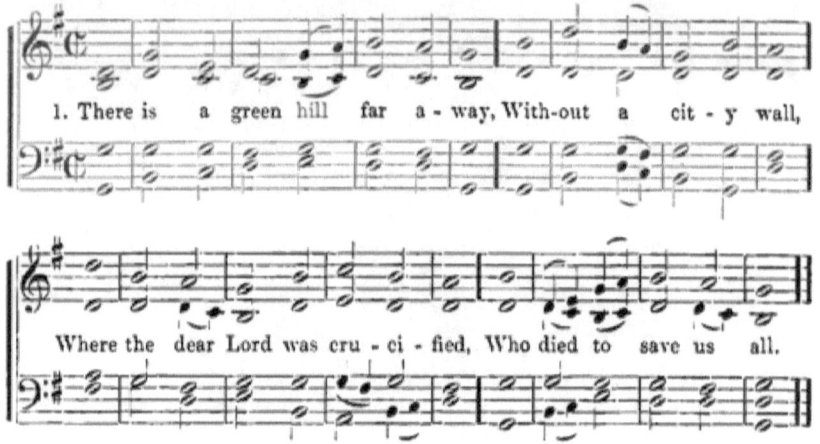

1. There is a green hill far a-way, With-out a cit-y wall, Where the dear Lord was cru-ci-fied, Who died to save us all.

2 We may not know, we cannot tell,
What pains He had to bear;
But we believe it was for us,
He hung and suffered there.

3 He died that we might be forgiven,
He died to make us good;
That we might go at last to heaven,
Saved by His precious blood.

4 There was no other, good enough
To pay the price of sin;
He only, could unlock the gate
Of heaven, and let us in.

5 O, dearly, dearly has He loved,
And we must love Him too:
And trust in His redeeming blood,
And try His works to do.

127½ What Wondrous Love is This?

1. What wondrous love is this, O my soul, O my soul! What wondrous love is
2. He led me first to see What I was, what I was; He led me first to
3. Some said I'd soon give o'er, You shall see, you shall see; Some said I'd soon give

this, O my soul! What wondrous love is this That caused the Lord of bliss To
see What I was; He led me first to see My sin and mis-er-ry, And
o'er; You shall see. Three years have pass'd away Since I be-gan to pray, I

send this precious peace To my soul, to my soul, To send this precious peace To my soul?
then He set me free; Bless His name, bless His name, And then He set me free, Bless His
 [name.
love the Lord to-day, Bless His name, bless His name, I love the Lord to-day, Bless
 [His name.

128. Religion Makes Me Happy.

Dedicated to William **Drew**.

Arr. for "Rescue Songs."

Copyright, 1890, by H. H. Hadley.

129. There is a Fold Whence None Can Stray.

Dedicated to E. O. H.

For "Rescue Songs." Arr. L. H. Hayden.

130. Angels Hovering Round.

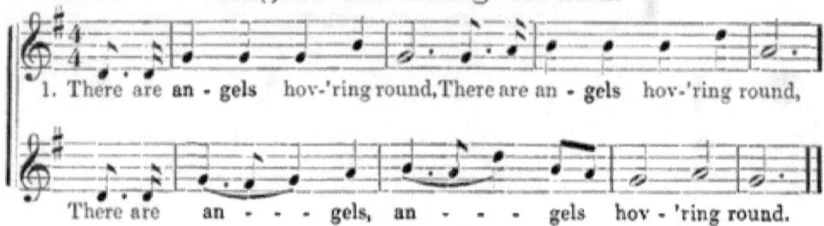

1. There are an-gels hov-'ring round, There are an-gels hov-'ring round,
There are an - - gels, an - - gels hov-'ring round.

2 To carry the tidings home.
3 To the New Jerusalem.
4 Poor sinners are coming home.
5 And Jesus bids them come.
6 Let him that heareth, come.
7 We are on our journey home.

131. Standing on the Promises.

R. K. C.   By per. JOHN J. HOOD.   R. KELSO CARTER.

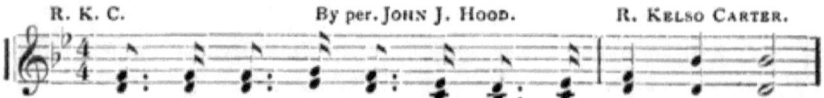

1 Standing on the promises of Christ my King,
Through eternal ages let His praises ring;
Glory in the highest, I will shout and sing,
Standing on the promises of God.

CHORUS.

Standing, Standing, Standing on the promises of God my Saviour:
Standing, Standing, I'm standing on the promises of God.

2 Standing on the promises that cannot fail,
When the howling storms of doubt and fears assail;
By the living Word of God I shall prevail,
Standing on the promises of God.—CHO.

3 Standing on the promises I now can see
Perfect, present cleansing in the blood for me;
Standing in the liberty where Christ makes free,
Standing on the promises of God.—CHO.

4 Standing on the promises of Christ the Lord,
Bound to Him eternally by love's strong cord,
Overcoming daily with the Spirit's sword,
Standing on the promises of God.—CHO.

5 Standing on the promises I cannot fall,
Listening every moment to the Spirit's call,
Resting in my Saviour, as my all in all,
Standing on the promises of God.—CHO.

Words and Music in "Precious Hymns." JOHN J. HOOD, Pub., Phila.

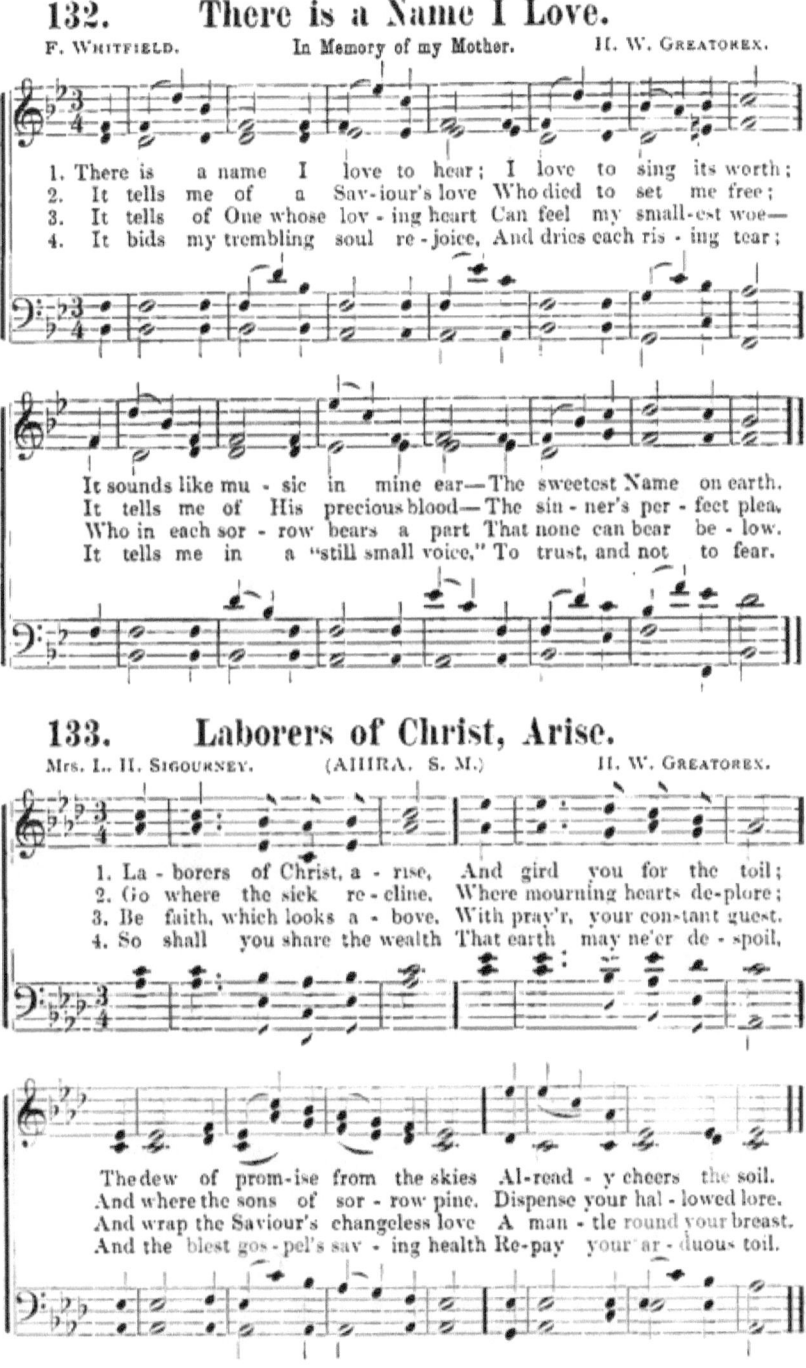

132. There is a Name I Love.

F. WHITFIELD.   In Memory of my Mother.   H. W. GREATOREX.

1. There is a name I love to hear; I love to sing its worth;
2. It tells me of a Sav-iour's love Who died to set me free;
3. It tells of One whose lov-ing heart Can feel my small-est woe—
4. It bids my trembling soul re-joice, And dries each ris-ing tear;

It sounds like mu-sic in mine ear—The sweetest Name on earth.
It tells me of His precious blood—The sin-ner's per-fect plea.
Who in each sor-row bears a part That none can bear be-low.
It tells me in a "still small voice," To trust, and not to fear.

133. Laborers of Christ, Arise.

Mrs. L. H. SIGOURNEY.   (AHIRA. S. M.)   H. W. GREATOREX.

1. La-borers of Christ, a-rise, And gird you for the toil;
2. Go where the sick re-cline, Where mourning hearts de-plore;
3. Be faith, which looks a-bove, With pray'r, your con-stant guest.
4. So shall you share the wealth That earth may ne'er de-spoil,

The dew of prom-ise from the skies Al-read-y cheers the soil.
And where the sons of sor-row pine, Dispense your hal-lowed lore.
And wrap the Saviour's changeless love A man-tle round your breast.
And the blest gos-pel's sav-ing health Re-pay your ar-duous toil.

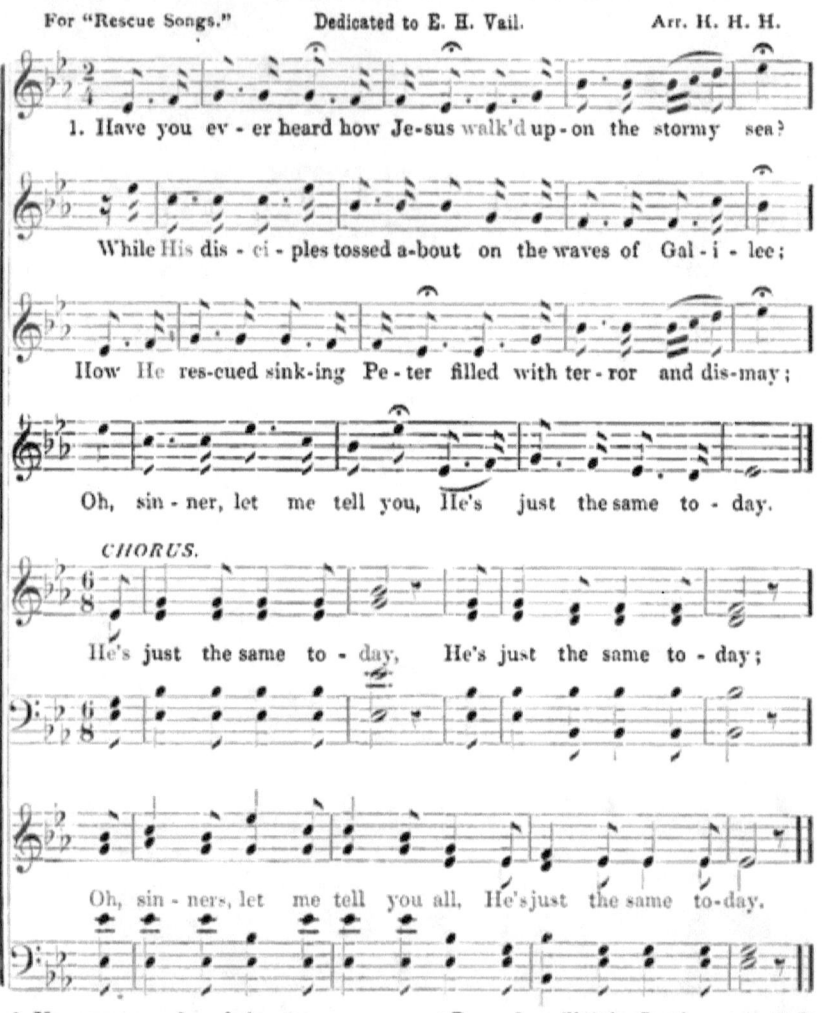

2 Have you ever heard the story
   Of the babe of Bethlehem?
  Who was worshiped by the angels
   And the wise and holy men?
  How He taught the learned doctors
   In the temple far away,
  Oh, sinners let me tell you,
   He is just the same to-day.

3 Once while resting on a pillow,
   In the vessel fast asleep,
  There arose a mighty tempest,
   On the wild and angry deep;

"Peace, be still." the Lord commanded,
   Every angry wave did stay.
  I am glad to tell you, sinners,
   He is just the same to-day.

4 Surely you have heard how Jesus
   Prayed down in Gethsemane,
  How He shed His precious life-blood
   On the rugged shameful tree,
  Cruel thorns His forehead piercing,
   As His Spirit passed away;
  Sinner, won't you come and love Him?
   For He is just the same to-day.

137. Onward, Christian Soldiers.

"Be strong and of good courage."—DEUT. 31: 6.

S. BARING—GOULD. A. S. SULLIVAN.

Hallelujah for the Cross. Concluded.

* For a final ending, all the voices may sing the melody in unison through the last eight measures—the instrument playing the harmony.

140. Noah and the Wine.

HENRY H. HADLEY.   Arr. by E. E. B.

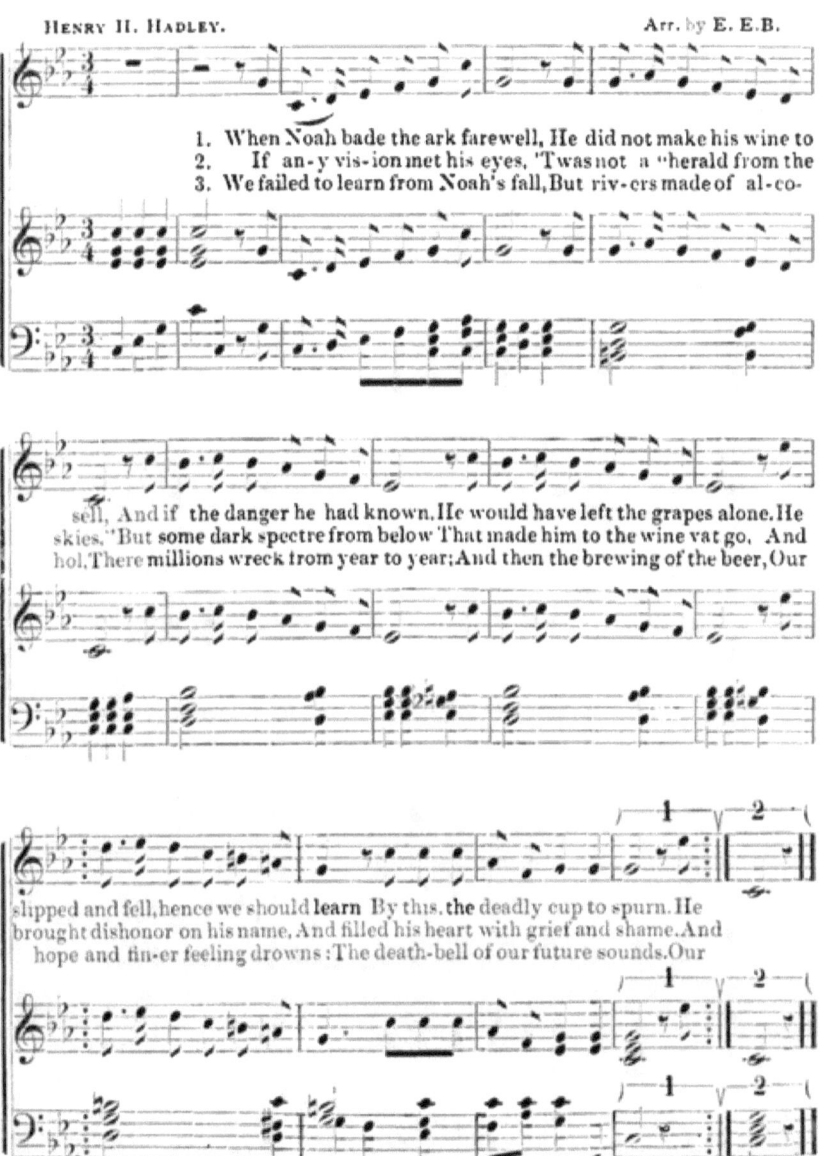

1. When Noah bade the ark farewell, He did not make his wine to sell, And if the danger he had known, He would have left the grapes alone. He slipped and fell, hence we should learn By this, the deadly cup to spurn. He
2. If an-y vis-ion met his eyes, 'Twas not a "herald from the skies," But some dark spectre from below That made him to the wine vat go. And brought dishonor on his name, And filled his heart with grief and shame. And
3. We failed to learn from Noah's fall, But riv-ers made of al-co-hol, There millions wreck from year to year; And then the brewing of the beer, Our hope and fin-er feeling drowns: The death-bell of our future sounds. Our

4 While they who now this work pursue,
Are victims oft to their own brew,
We too must share their hapless fate,
If we their habits imitate.
The gallows-tree and prison pen,
Show where the fiend too oft hath been.

5 But there's a refuge for the lost
That our Redeemer's blood hath cost;
He offers now to you and me,
Redemption full redemption free.
Oh seek Him while He may be found,
Let home and heaven with joy resound.

Copyright, 1890, by H. H. HADLEY.

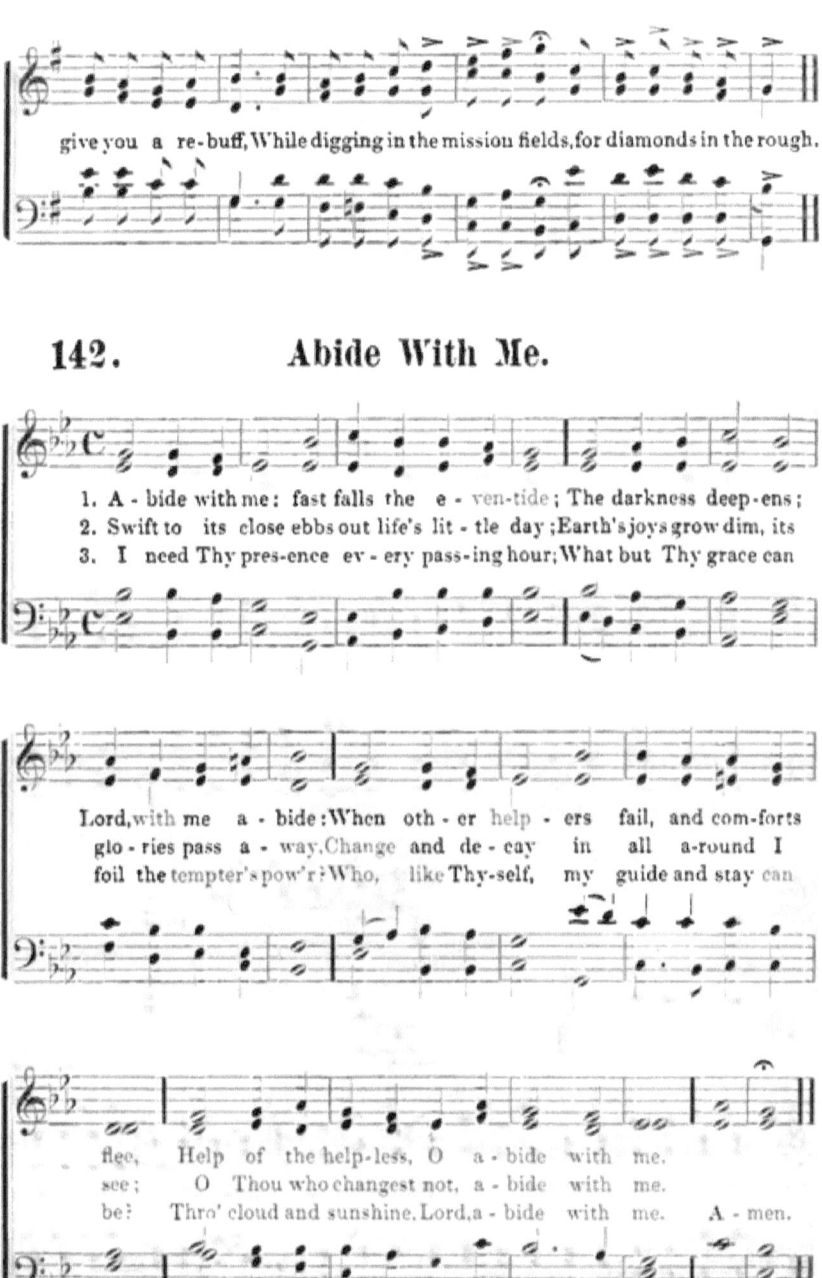

The Master Stood in His Garden. Concluded.

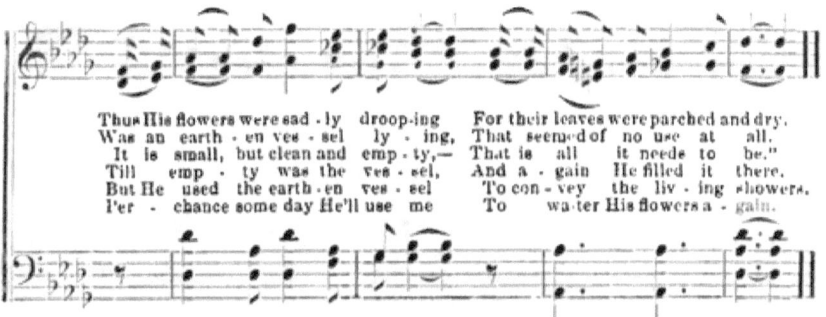

Thus His flowers were sad-ly droop-ing For their leaves were parched and dry.
Was an earth-en ves-sel ly-ing, That seemed of no use at all.
It is small, but clean and emp-ty,— That is all it needs to be."
Till emp-ty was the ves-sel, And a-gain He filled it there.
But He used the earth-en ves-sel To con-vey the liv-ing showers.
Per-chance some day He'll use me To wa-ter His flowers a-gain.

144. A Little Talk With Jesus.

TUNE:—*Traced her little footsteps in the snow.*

1 While fighting for my Saviour here,
   The devil tries me hard:
He uses all his mighty power,
   My progress to retard:
He's up to every move,
And yet through all I prove,
   A little talk with Jesus makes it right.

CHORUS.

A little talk with Jesus makes it right, all right;
   Through trials of every kind,
   Praise God I always find,
   A little talk with Jesus makes it right.

2 Tho' dark the night and clouds look black
   And stormy overhead:
And trials of most every kind
   Across my path are spread;
How soon I conquer all
As to the Lord I call,
   A little talk with Jesus makes it right.

4 And thus, by frequent little talks,
   I gain the victory;
And march along with cheerful song,
   Enjoying liberty;
With Jesus as my Friend
I'll prove until the end,
   A little talk with Jesus makes it right.

145. Hallelujah! Jesus Saves.

HENRY H. HADLEY.   Arr. L. H. HAYDEN.

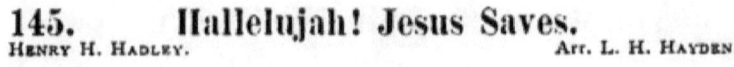

1. While I in sin was wand'ring, I heard the glad re-frain,
My heart ech-oed the tid-ings, And sent it back a-gain,
But O, this news so wonderful, Has brightened up the road,

Hallelujah! Jesus saves. All hail! He saves. Hal-le-lu-jah! Jesus saves.

For years in sin and sor-row I strug-gled with my load;

2 I've told the news to others,
It made their hearts rejoice,
Hallelujah! etc.
Like me they heard Him calling,
And hastened at His voice;
Hallelujah! etc.
When Satan heard he trembled,
And let the fetters go;
So they are safe within the fold,
And all the world shall know.
Hallelujah! etc.

3 Now as the mount I'm climbing,
I'll sing the Heav'nly strain;
Hallelujah! etc.
The angels hear the music,
And answer back again;
Hallelujah! etc.
At last in Heaven rejoicing,
When I His face behold;
I'll sing through endless ages,
Along the streets of gold;
Hallelujah! etc.

Copyright. 1890, by H. H. HADLEY.

146. Sometimes.

1. A mix-ture of joy and sor-row, I dai-ly do pass through;
Sometimes I'm in the val-ley, A sinking down with woe.
I view by faith bright Ca-naan, And stand up-on its shore.

Sometimes I am ex-alt-ed, On ea-gle's wings I soar;

2 Sometimes I'm sorely tempted,
And filled with doubt and fear;
Then when I look to Jesus,
He always will come near.

Sometimes I go to meeting,
And wish I'd stay'd at home;
Sometimes I meet my Saviour.
And then I'm glad I've come.

147. Where is my Father To-night.

CARRIE MERRES.   AIR.—"Where is my Wandering Boy?"

1 Where has my father gone to-night?
   The father I love so well;
   He wanders away from home and friends;
   My sorrow no words can tell.

CHO.—O where is my sire to-night?
   O where can my father be?
   I love him yet, and I cannot forget
   My mother's last words to me.

2 Once we could say our home was bright,
   As we knelt at his knee for prayer;
   No face more kind, no heart more true—
   None loved us with fonder care.—CHO.

3 I stood and watched by her dying bed,
   And softly she said to me,
   "I feel that our prayers will yet be heard;
   Your father reclaimed will be."—CHO.

4 Go to my wand'ring sire to-night,
   And tell him the words of love,
   That I may hope we'll meet again
   On earth, or with mother above.—CHO.

Copyright, 1890, by H. H. HADLEY.

148. You're Saving a Man.

Rev. F. BOTTOME, D.D.   AIR.—"Star Spangled Banner."

1 O see the poor drunkard, so lost to all shame,
   So dead to all sense of the sin that is in him;
   Rouse him up, if you can, by that Wonderful Name,
   And then watch till you see the new life stir within him.

CHO.—‖: Then up to the rescue, and save if you can;
   Remember, good brother, you're saving a man! :‖

2 What a fall from the joy and the beauty of youth!
   What a wreck of desire and young hope's aspiring;
   What a fearful destruction of virtue and truth!—
   Nothing left but the victim in sadness expiring.—CHO.

3 And, alas! for the desolate household and home,
   For the laughter of childhood now turned into wailing;
   For the smiles and contentment that never can come,—
   For the heart-broken wife in her pleas unavailing.—CHO.

4 Go then in His name to the brink of the grave
   And shout till the dead in their caverns awaking,
   Shall rise in the life of the mighty to save,
   And shine in the light of the morning's new breaking.—CHO.

152. Save, Oh, Save!

Show pit - y, Lord, O Lord, for - give! Save, bless-ed Sav - iour,
D.S.—Save, bless-ed Sav - iour,

Let a re - pent-ing reb - el live; Save, mighty Lord.   Save, oh, save!
And send con-vert-ing pow-er down; Save, mighty Lord.

153. Speak to Them, Lord.

Jerry made the first prayer. I shall never forget it. He said: "Dear Saviour, won't you look down in pity on these poor souls? They need your help, Lord, they can't get along without it. Blessed Jesus, these poor sinners have got themselves into a bad hole. Won't you help them out? Speak to them, Lord! do, for Jesus' sake—Amen!"—From "*My First Drink and My Last.*" By S. H. Hadley, Jerry's successor. Fleming H. Revell, New York, Pub.

Jerry said: "All the prayers in the world won't save you unless you pray for yourself." I halted but a moment, and then, with a breaking heart, I said: "*Dear Jesus, can you help me?*" Never with mortal tongue can I describe that moment. I felt the glorious brightness shine into my heart; I felt I was a free man. (See No. 67.)

Dedicated to the Memory of Jerry McAuley.

Words by FANNY J. CROSBY.   TUNE.—"Autumn." For "Rescue Songs."

1 Lord, behold in Thy compassion,
   Those who kneel before Thee now;
  They are in a sad condition,
   None can help them, Lord, but Thou.

CHORUS.

  Speak to them in tender mercy;
   Now their cruel fetters break;
  "Speak to them," we humbly pray Thee,
   Do, O Lord, for Jesus' sake.

2 They are lost, but do not leave them,
   In their dreary path to roam;
  There is pardon, precious pardon,
   If to Thee by faith they come.—CHO.

3 They are lost, but do not leave them,
   In the pit so dark and cold;
  Take them out and kindly bear them,
   Like a shepherd to the fold.—CHO.

4 Thou dost know their every feeling,
   Their temptations Thou canst see;
  Here they are, O Lord, receive them,
   As they give themselves to Thee.—CHO.

154. At the Cross I'll Abide.

I. B.   "And many women were there."—MATT. 27: 55.   I. BALTZELL.

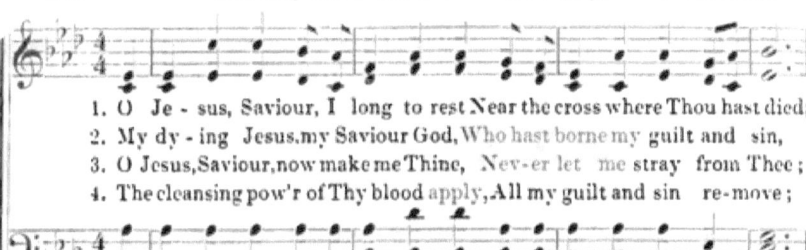

1. O Jesus, Saviour, I long to rest Near the cross where Thou hast died;
2. My dying Jesus, my Saviour God, Who hast borne my guilt and sin,
3. O Jesus, Saviour, now make me Thine, Never let me stray from Thee;
4. The cleansing pow'r of Thy blood apply, All my guilt and sin remove;

For there is hope for the aching breast, At the cross I will abide.
Now wash me, cleanse me with Thine own blood, Ever keep me pure and clean.
Oh, wash me, cleanse me, for Thou art mine, And Thy love is full and free.
Oh, help me, while at Thy cross I lie, Fill my soul with perfect love.

CHORUS.

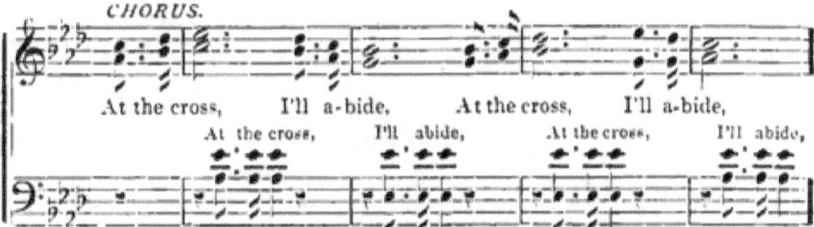

At the cross, I'll abide, At the cross, I'll abide,

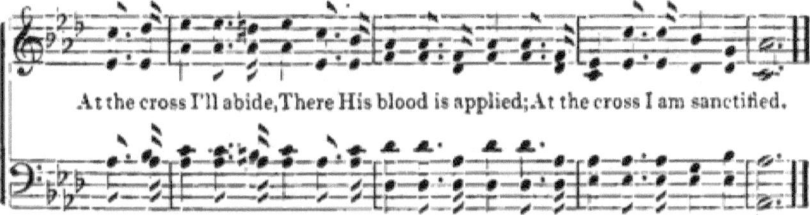

At the cross I'll abide, There His blood is applied; At the cross I am sanctified.

By permission.

155. There is a Fountain.

W. Cowper.   Lowell Mason.

1. There is a foun-tain filled with blood, Drawn from Im-man-uel's veins, And sin-ners plung'd beneath that flood Lose all their guilt-y stains. Lose all their guilt-y stains Lose all their guilt-y stains;

2 The dying thief rejoiced to see
   That fountain in his day;
And there may I, though vile as he,
   Wash all my sins away.

3 Dear dying Lamb, Thy precious blood
   Shall never lose its power,
Till all the ransomed church of God
   Be saved to sin no more.

4 E'er since, by faith, I saw the stream
   Thy flowing wounds supply,
Redeeming love has been my theme,
   And shall be, till I die.

5 Then in a nobler, sweeter song,
   I'll sing Thy power to save,
When this poor lisping, stam'ring tongue
   Lies silent in the grave.

156. The Backslider.

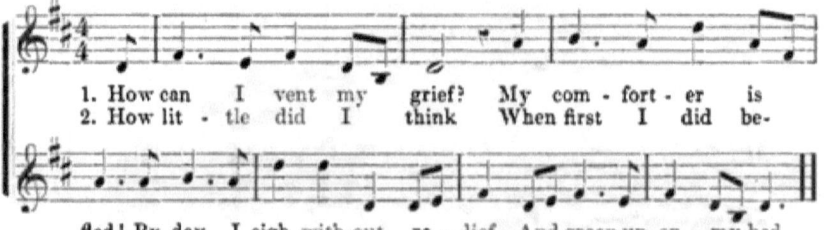

1. How can I vent my grief? My com-fort-er is fled! By day I sigh with-out re-lief And groan up-on my bed.
2. How lit-tle did I think When first I did be-gin To join a lit-tle with the world It was so great a sin.

3 My confidence is gone,
   I find no words to say,
Barren and lifeless is my soul
   When I attempt to pray

4 Trembling, to Christ I'll fly,
   And all my sins confess,
At Jesus' cross I'll humbly fall
   And ask restoring grace.

157. When I Set Out for Glory.

1. When I set out for glo-ry I left the world behind, De-ter-mined for a cit-y That's out of sight to find.

CHORUS.
And to glo-ry I will go, And to glo-ry I will go, I'll go, I'll go, And to glo-ry I will go!

158. MY TRUNDLE BED.

1 As I rumaged through the attic,
　Listening to the falling rain,
As it pattered on the shingles,
　And against the window pane;
Peeping over chests and boxes,
　Which with dust were thickly spread,
Saw I in the farthest corner,
　What was once my trundle bed.

2 So I drew it from the recess,
　Where it had remained so long,
Hearing all the while the music
　Of my mother's voice in song,
As she sung in sweetest accents,
　What I since have often read:
"Hush, my dear, lie still and slumber;
　Holy Angels guard thy bed."

3 As I listened, recollections
　That I thought had been forgot,
Came with all the gush of memory,
　Rushing, thronging to the spot;
And I wandered back to childhood
　To those merry days of yore,
When I knelt beside my mother,
　By that bed upon the floor.

4 Then it was, with hands so gently
　Placed upon my infant head,
That she taught my lips to utter,
　Carefully the words she said.
Never can they be forgotten;
　Deep are they in memory riven:
"Hallowed be Thy name, Oh, Father!
　Father, Thou who art in heaven."

5 This she taught me; then she told me
　Of its import great and deep;
After which I learned to utter,
　"Now I lay me down to sleep."
Then it was with hands uplifted,
　And in accents soft and mild,
That my mother asked our Father,
　"Father, do Thou bless my child."

6 Years have passed, and that dear mother
　Long has mouldered 'neath the sod,
And I know her sainted spirit
　Dwells within the home of God.
But that scene in summer twilight,
　Fills my heart with joy divine,
For my mother's prayer is answered,
　And her Saviour now is mine.

159. IF PAPA WERE ONLY READY.

1 I should like to die, said Willie,
　If my papa could die too,
But he says he isn't ready,
　'Cause he has so much to do;
And little sister Nellie says,
　That I must surely die,
And that she and mamma—then she stopped
　Because it made me cry.

2 But she told me, I remember,
　Once while sitting on her knee,
That the angels never weary,
　Watching over her and me;
And that if we're good—and mamma told me
　Just the same before—
They will let us into Heaven,
　When they see us at the door.

3 There I know I shall be happy,
　And will always want to stay;
I shall love to hear the singing,
　I shall love the endless day;
I shall love to look at Jesus,
　I shall love Him more and more;
And I'll gather water lilies
　For the angel at the door.

4 There will be none but the holy,
　I shall know no more of sin,
I will see mamma and Nellie,
　For I know He'll let them in;
But I'll have to tell the angel,
　When I meet Him at the door,
That He must excuse my papa,
　'Cause he couldn't leave the store.

5 Nellie says that may be
　I shall soon be called away;
If papa was only ready,
　I should like to go to-day;
But if I should go before him
　To that world of light and joy,
Then I guess he'd want to come to Heaven
　To see his little boy.

161. Glad Tidings.

M. E. W.
Mrs. M. E. Wilson.

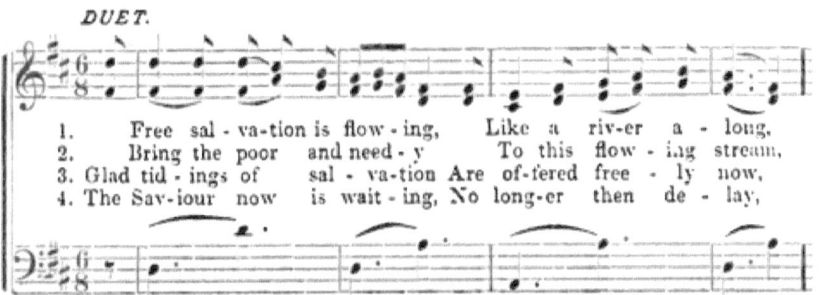

1. Free salvation is flowing, Like a river along,
2. Bring the poor and needy To this flowing stream,
3. Glad tidings of salvation Are offered freely now,
4. The Saviour now is waiting, No longer then delay,

O-ver mountain and valley, And this is our song:
Tell them Christ is able, And waiting to redeem:
Accept the invitation; To Jesus humbly bow:
Believe, accept, and trust Him; And be saved today.

CHORUS.

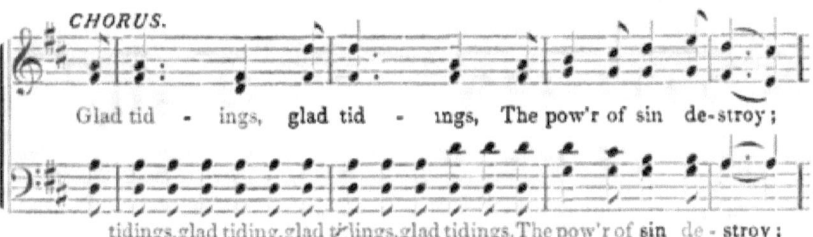

Glad tidings, glad tidings, The pow'r of sin destroy;
tidings, glad tiding, glad tidings, glad tidings, The pow'r of sin destroy;

Glad tidings, glad tidings, Glad tidings of great joy.

Copyright, 1885, by Mrs. M. E. Wilson. By per. From "Great Joy" by per.

162. I Have Tried the World.

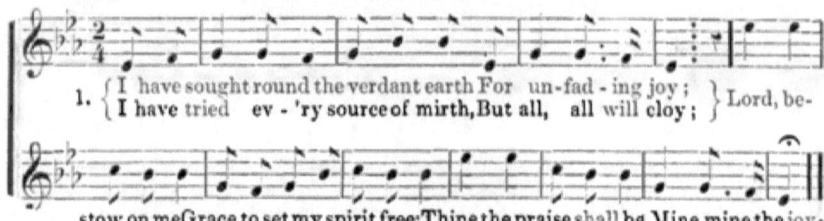

1. { I have sought round the verdant earth For un-fad-ing joy;
    I have tried ev-'ry source of mirth, But all, all will cloy; } Lord, bestow on me Grace to set my spirit free; Thine the praise shall be, Mine, mine the joy.

2 I have wandered in mazes dark
    Of doubt and distress;
  I have had not a kindling spark,
    My sprit to bless;
  Cheerless unbelief
  Filled my lab'ring soul with grief;
  What shall give relief?
    What shall give peace?

3 Then I turned to Thy gospel, Lord,
    From folly away;
  Then I trusted Thy Holy Word
    That taught me to pray;
  Here I found release—
  In Thy Word my soul found peace,
  Hope of endless bliss,
    Eternal day.

4 I will praise now my heavenly King,
    I'll praise and adore;
  All my heart's richest tribute bring
    To Thee, God of power;
  And in heaven above,
  Saved by Thy redeeming love,
  Loud the strains shall move
    For evermore.

163. Back to My Mission Home.

F. J. C.   For "Rescue Songs."

TUNE.—"I Wandered by the Brookside."

1 I had wandered from the mission, where like a summer day,
    Without a cloud or shadow many months had passed away;
  And with heedless step I entered where oft I'd been before,
    But the tempter had preceded me and met me at the door.

2 Then I took the hands extended and drank the proffered cheer,
    I joined their evening revels, too, but was not happy there;
  And soon o'er what was passing my thoughts had ceased to roam,
    For a music-box was playing the air of "Home, Sweet Home."

TUNE.—"There's no place like Home."

3 It swept o'er my spirit till sadly I wept,
    It wakened the chords that a moment had slept;
  I felt like a wand'rer o'er ocean's dark foam,
    But Hope said, "Return to thy dear Mission Home."

CHO.—Home, Home, sweet, sweet home,
    No place in the world like my dear Mission Home.

4 It swept o'er my spirit, that music so sweet,
    And brought me again to the dear Saviour's feet;
  O Jesus, no more from Thy side will I roam,
    But ever abide in my dear Mission Home.—CHO.

Copyright, 1890, by H. H. Hadley.

164. Keep me, Lord, low down.

Arr. by J. P. W.

1. I know my sins are all for-giv'n, Carry me to the promis'd land, where
2. Poor sin-ner, you may be set free, Carry me to the promis'd land, where
3. I do re-joice for him I sing, Carry me to the promis'd land, where
4. My Sav-iour bore my sins a-way, Carry me to the promis'd land, where

pleasures never die, And I am on my way to heav'n, Car-ry me to the
pleasures never die, For you he died on Cal-va-ry, Car-ry me to the
pleasures never die, My Saviour comes, I reign with him, Car-ry me to the
pleasures never die, And I will praise him night and day, Car-ry me to the

REFRAIN.

promis'd land where pleasures never die. Keep me, Lord, low down, till I
promis'd land where pleasures never die.
promis'd land where pleasures never die.
promis'd land where pleasures never die.

die, Oh, car-ry me to the promis'd land, Where pleasures never die.

Copyright, 1886, by E. E. Nickerson.

167. Satisfied.

Miss Clara Teare.   R. E. Hudson.

1. All my life long I had pant-ed For a draught from some cool spring
2. Feeding on the husks a-round me, Till my strength was al-most gone,
3. Poor I was, and sought for rich-es, Something that would sat-is-fy,
4. Well of wa-ter, ev-er springing, Bread of life, so rich and free,

That I hop'd would quench the burning, Of the thirst I felt with-in.
Long'd my soul for something bet-ter, On-ly still to hun-ger on.
But the dust I gath-ered round me On-ly mock'd my soul's sad cry.
Un-told wealth that nev-er fail-eth, My Re-deem-er is to me.

CHORUS.

Hal-le-lu-jah! I have found Him—Whom my soul so long has crav'd!

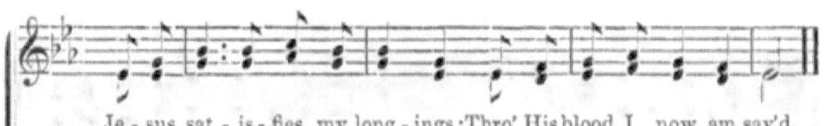

Je-sus sat-is-fies my long-ings; Thro' His blood I now am sav'd.

Used by permission.

169. Mighty to Save.

G. W. S.
G. W. SEDERQUIST.

"I that speak in righteousness, mighty to save."—Isa. 63: 1.

1. Say, why do you linger so long in sin, When Je-sus is mighty to save?
2. Come leave the broad road, and the good way choose, For Jesus is mighty to save;
3. As time is fast fleeting, 'twill soon be gone, But Je-sus is mighty to save;

O turn to him now, and the new life begin, For Je-sus is mighty to save.
The gospel of power proclaims the **good news** That Jesus is mighty to save.
He gently invites **thee** to learn the new song, That Jesus is mighty to **save.**

CHORUS.

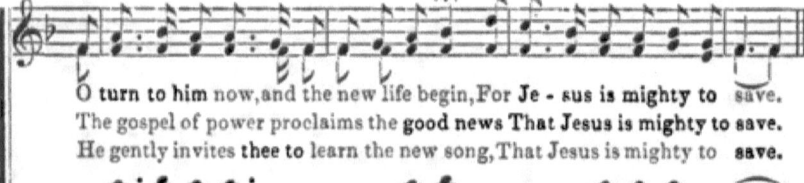

Come, ... Come, ...
O why not come to him now?.... O why not come to him now?....
Just now, Just now.

O come and believe, free pardon receive, For Je-sus is mighty to save.

4
While mercy is calling, O come and see
That Jesus is mighty to save;
Full pardon is offered, salvation is free,
And Jesus is mighty to save.—*Cho.*

5
Come now, while we're praying, we plead
And Jesus is waiting to save. [for thee,
O haste to the refuge, to Jesus now **flee**,
For he will abundantly **save**.—*Cho.*

Copyright, 1886, by J. HEMENWAY.

INDEX TO HYMNS.

	No.		No.
Abide with me	142	I am saved	134
Abiding	91	I believe Jesus saves	5
A hundred years ago	160	I can, I will, I do believe	159
A little talk with Jesus	144	If papa were only ready	109
A mighty league of prayer	125	I gave up nothing	76
Angels hovering round	130	I'll bear it, Lord, for Thee	100
Art thou weary	65	I'll feed on husks no more	64
A shout in the camp	4	I'm going home to die no more	87
At the cross	165	I'm resting at last	168
At the cross I'll abide	154	I own I'm base	79½
Away over Jordan	26	I've tried the world	162
		I will follow Jesus	95
Back to my mission home	163	I will shout His praise in glory	41
Backward, turn backward	86	I yield to Thee	33
Bear the cross for Jesus	36		
Burst ye emerald gates	3	Jesus bids you come	35
		Jesus of Nazareth passeth by	108
Come, sinner, come	2	Jesus took me by the hand	116
Come to Jesus just now	61		
Come to the feast	139	Keep me from sinking down	20
Companionship with Jesus	28	Keep me, Lord, low down	164
Consolation	24	Keep off temptation ground	79
Crown Him	71		
		Laborers of Christ, arise	133
Dear Jesus, canst Thou help me	67	Lead, kindly light	55
Diamonds in the rough	141	Lead me gently home, Father	34
Don't sell my father rum	72	Let Jesus walk the waves to thee	7
		Look not in the sparkling wine	119
Entire consecration	105	Look not on the rosy wine	114½
For you and for me	69		
		Medley of choruses	98
Gather them in	112	Memories of Galilee	47
Glad tidings	161	Mighty to save	169
Glorious morning	121	Mount Calvary	66
Glory to God! hallelujah	48	Move forward	9
Glory to His name	89	My beautiful home	122
God be with you	170	My brethren I have found	6
God's promises	97	My telegram's gone	120
		My trundle bed	158
Hallelujah for the cross	138		
Hallelujah! Jesus saves	145	Naaman the Leper	19
Happy tidings	94	Never go back again	49
He is calling	50	Noah and the wine	140
He loved me	45	Nothing pays but serving God	150
He rose	32	Now I feel the sacred fire	63
He saves the drunkard too	113	Now will I tell	151
He's just the same to-day	136		
Hours that are fleeting away	51		

INDEX TO HYMNS.

Title	No.
O happy day	22
Oh for a heart to praise my God	37½
Oh, how sweet at Jesus' feet	18
Oh! the Lamb	114
Oh! 'tis glory in my soul	37
Onward, Christian soldiers	137
O sing of His mighty love	40
Our standard	62
Overcomers	92
Please let my mother go	84
Redeemed, praise the Lord	10
Redemption	15
Religion makes me happy	128
Rescue song	88
Rescue the sinner	90
Rest for the weary	73
Rest in the Lord	81
Ring the bells	104
Royal way of the cross	13
Satisfied	167
Save, oh, save	152
Shall I be saved to-night	29
Shall we meet	102
She is coming home to-morrow	60
Since I have been redeemed	77
Sinner, see yon light	30
Sometimes	146
Sound the battle cry	44
Sowing the tares	54
Speak, Lord	101
Speak to them, Lord	153
Standing on the promises	131
Steal away	56
Step out on the promise	31
Sweet peace, the gift of God's love	75
Swing low, sweet chariot	68
Submission	96
Take the whole armour	70
Tell it again	135
Tell it to Jesus alone	123
That old, old story is true	74
The angels are looking on me	166
The backslider	156
The beautiful city of gold	58
The best of books	110

Title	No.
The bleeding Lamb	52
The child of a King	103
The cross	38
The first Psalm	107
The garden of the Lord	57
The gracious call	14
The King's son	111
The lily of the valley	11
The Lord will provide	39
The Master stood in His garden	143
The new "over there"	118
The new song	23
The old time religion	115
There is a fold whence none can stray	129
There is a fountain	155
There is a green hill far away	127
There is a name I love	132
There is a time	106
There's something more than gold	53
The Rock that is higher than I	59
The Shepherd of the sheep	99
The sinner and the song	93
The volunteer's song	1
The waters of Jordan may roll	124
Thou art a mighty Saviour	42
'Tis some mother's child	85
Try him for twenty-four hours	83
Trust me	126
Valley of blessing	17
Wait a little while	46
Waiting at the pool	78
Weep for the fallen	12
Welcome for me	25
We're on the way	149
We walk by faith	21
What's the news	80
What wondrous love is this	127½
When I set out for glory	157
When peace like a river	27
Where is my father to-night	147
Where the living waters flow	8
While the years are rolling on	43
Willing workers	82
Whosoever will may come	16
Why I love Jesus	117
You're saving a man	148

NEW — APPROPRIATE — POPULAR.

FOR USE IN RESCUE MISSIONS
AND
OTHER RELIGIOUS SERVICES.

RESCUE Songs

WORDS AND MUSIC

With Standard Selections.

BY

COL. H. H. HADLEY.

S. T. GORDON & SON, Publishers,
No. 13 E. 14th St.,
NEW YORK.

Heavy Paper Covers, by mail, postpaid, per copy, 20 cents; by express, charges not prepaid, $15 per hundred. Board Covers, by mail, postpaid, per copy, 25 cents; by express, charges not prepaid, $20 per hundred.

FOR SALE BY ALL MUSIC DEALERS AND BOOKSELLERS.

SEND FOR A PLEDGE CARD AT ONCE!

PLEDGE TO BECOME A RESCUE VOLUNTEER.

In becoming an Auxiliary Rescue Volunteer, I agree to *seek the acquaintance of one slave to alcohol, and for one year do all in my power to* WIN *him or her to renounce drink and lead a Christian life, and to* pray each day for the success of all Rescue Missions in reclaiming drunkards, and especially for the success of the efforts of the RESCUE VOLUNTEERS in this work.

Name...

Address......................................

Date................

N. B.—*For children and youths* and special cases who cannot conscientiously agree to that part of the pledge which is in Italics, please cross that out.

When this pledge is signed please mail it at once to

Yours in His Name,

H. H. HADLEY,

158 E. 42d Street, NEW YORK.

HOW TO DO IT.

WIN by prayerful, patient perseverance and acts of kindness.
Never argue, scold or reproach.
Forgive and welcome back until he or she falls 490 times (seventy times seven).
By saving from *Sin* you RESCUE from *Drink.* Present Christ as the *perfect Saviour.*
"Be it known unto you that by the name of Jesus Christ of Nazareth, even by him doth this man stand before you whole.
"For there is none other name under heaven given among men whereby we *must be saved.*"

RESCUE VOLUNTEER BADGE.

This is the true size and style of our beautiful Solid Silver badge. A silver ring goes through the closed slot above in half of them for those who wish them to hang as a charm. Half of them are furnished with a two inch pin for the scarf.

To become a Volunteer you do not have to buy a badge. Only sign and return the pledge card. But if you want a Badge, here is the prettiest one yet made, we think, and will be mailed to the address of anyone who signs this pledge, on receipt of 25 cents.

To Pastors, Evangelists, Gospel Singers, and Sunday School Superintendents.

We desire to call your attention to our new work

PEARLS OF GOSPEL SONG
—BY—
WM. A. OGDEN AND WARREN W. BENTLEY,

and containing special contributions from many of the best Gospel Song Writers of the day.

Pearls of Gospel Song is in every respect fully equal to the very best Selections of Gospel Songs now in use, having been prepared and selected after long experience in practical use of the Gospel Songs which have been so popular during the past ten years.

The Songs now presented have the advantage of being **new**, thoroughly evangelical, and suited to every department of religious work.

Pearls of Gospel Song is printed in large clear type, fine paper, strongly bound, and will be furnished at the following prices:

Paper Covers, ...25 cts. each,	....$20.00 per 100 copies.
Board " ....30 "	" .... 25.00 " "
Cloth, flexible,...50 "	" .... 45.00 " "
Cloth and Gilt, ..75 "	" .... 60.00 " "

Specimen pages free.

Do not supply your Church or Sunday School until you have examined this book.

Address all orders to Publishers.

S. T. GORDON & SON,
No. 13 East 14th Street.

Copyright, 1884, by S. T. Gordon & Son.

www.ingramcontent.com/pod-product-compliance
Lightning Source LLC
Chambersburg PA
CBHW030251170426
43202CB00009B/705